SCIENCE AND HEALTH	MATHEMATICS	FINE ARTS
Atmosphere, Solar System, Clouds, Rain, Snow, Climate, Machines	Telling Time Types of Clocks	Listen to Music Box Compare to Chiming Clock Architectural Beauty
Maps Chart Making	Cost of Publishing and Distributing Newspaper	Patriotic Songs (Civil War Songs) Illustrations for Class Newspaper
Study Telescope Star Mythology	Distance	Negro Spirituals in History
Inventor Machines (shoe) History of Shoes	Importance of Math in Inventions	Listen to record on Sound, Machine, Rhythm, Noise, etc.
Study of Minerals Study of Salt	Money; Counting; Thrift	Mural of Life
Use of Thermometer Study of Body and how it works First Aid	Study of Symbols (degrees) Fractions and Decimals	Make booklet depicting his life
Study of Colors	Measurement and Perimeter (picture frames)	Relate Art and Music Appreciation Paint picture depicting some portion of his life
Study of Plants Use of Microscope Laboratory Experiments	Liquid Measurements Dry Measurements	Write booklet describing his life from child to manhood
Study of Heat & Cold	Maps Charting Longitude Latitude	Diorama of Eskimo life Songs about Eskimos
Study of Science of Sound	Fractions (musical notes)	Illustrate Songs

AFRO-AMERICAN CONTRIBUTORS TO AMERICAN LIFE

John Fitzgerald Kennedy said, "We can not neglect the great American contributors to American life."

In the quest for a positive racial identity, some Americans of color prefer the term Negro or black. There are others who choose to be called Afro-Americans because it denotes the ancestry of a race of people.

Discussing a race of people in their proper perspective involves looking at the beginning of the man. This race of man had its beginnings in Africa. However, most Afro-Americans, having been born in the United States are Americans first and Afro's second.

The City School District of Rochester had been concerned with the lack of materials on minority groups who have helped make America great. Thus, Project Beacon was initiated to develop materials intended to be used by all children, so that all students may learn of the many contributions made by the various minority individuals and groups.

Project Beacon is a cooperative program between the City School District of Rochester and Project Able, Division of Pupil Personnel Services, New York State Education Department.

Grateful acknowledgment is made to the following publishers for permission to reprint, on the pages indicated, excerpts from the publications named:

page 90: from *Yet Do I Marvel*, by Countee Cullen, Harper & Row, 1963. page 98: from *Understanding Other Cultures*, by Ina C. Brown, Prentice Hall, Inc., 1963. page 114: from *For My People*, by Langston Hughes, Alfred A. Knopf, Inc., 1926.

AFRO-AMERICAN CONTRIBUTORS TO AMERICAN LIFE

Senior Author
John M. Franco

Consultant
Dr. Walter M. Lifton

Writers
Suzanne Shade
Katherine Logan
Kaleen Sherman
Bevell Mason
Joan Kelley
Carl Mitchell
Mary Corris
Mary Ellen Delehanty
Velma Gladstone
Diane Henry
Gloria Huddleston
Eunice Leary
Carol Miller
Patrick Mulich
Diane Rinaldo
Marva Smith
Andrea Wolfe

Contributors
Ruth Anderson
Shirley Aroesty
Vivian Brennan
Susan Epstein
Norma Crittenden
Edward Delaney
Sylvia Levy
Frank Rinere

We are indebted to Dr. Alfred Stiller, former Director of Guidance, Rochester; and Herman R. Goldberg, Superintendent of Schools, Rochester, for their support, encouragement, and help in working on this project.

BENEFIC PRESS • WESTCHESTER, ILLINOIS

CONTENTS

BIOGRAPHY:

1. Benjamin Banneker (1731-1806) — 6
   Astronomer and Mathematician
2. Frederick Douglass (1817-1895) — 14
   Freedomfighter, Statesman, Editor
3. Harriet Tubman (1820-1913) — 24
   Led over 300 Slaves to Freedom
4. Jan E. Matzeliger (1852-1889) — 34
   Inventor
5. Booker T. Washington (1858-1915) — 40
   Educator
6. Daniel Hale Williams (1858-1931) — 48
   Physician
7. Henry Ossawa Tanner (1859-1937) — 56
   Artist
8. George Washington Carver (1864-1943) — 64
   Agricultural Chemist, Teacher
9. Matthew A. Henson (1866-1955) — 74
   Explorer
10. James Weldon Johnson (1871-1938) — 82
   Writer

Library of Congress
Number 74-94973

11. Paul Laurence Dunbar (1872-1906) 90
Lyric Poet
12. Mary McLeod Bethune (1875-1955) 98
Educator
13. Percy Lanon Julian (1899-) 106
Research Chemist
14. Langston Hughes (1902-1967) 114
Poet, Author
15. Charles Drew (1904-1950) 122
Pioneer in Preserving Blood
16. Ralph Bunche (1904-) 130
Statesman
17. Marian Anderson (1908-) 140
Concert Singer
18. Jackie Robinson (1919-) 148
Baseball Player
19. Martin Luther King, Jr. (1929-1968) 158
Fighter for Peace and Freedom,
Minister, Nobel Prize Winner
20. Willie Howard Mays (1931-) 166
Baseball Player

Landmarks and Milestones 176

Afro-American Contributors 184

Index 191

Acknowledgments 192

BENJAMIN BANNEKER
(1731-1806)
Astronomer and Mathematician

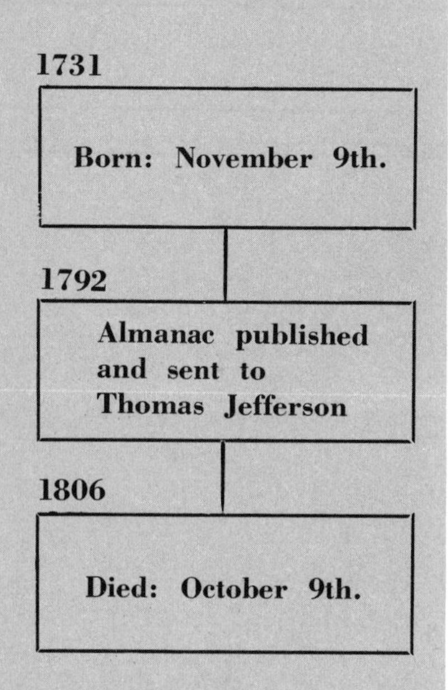

Nobody wishes more than I do to see such proofs as you exhibit, that nature has given to our black brethren, talents equal to those of the other colors of man, and that the appearance of a want of them is owing merely to the degraded condition of their existence, both in Africa and America.

Thomas Jefferson
Letter to Benjamin Banneker

MEETING BENJAMIN BANNEKER

Can you picture a little boy who liked to read more than he liked to play? This may be difficult to picture. However, there really was such a little boy. His name was Benjamin Banneker. He was born a long time ago on a farm near Baltimore, Maryland.

One day, Benjamin borrowed a watch from a friend. He took the watch apart to see how it worked. He then studied it for a long, long time.

"I would like to make a clock," said Benjamin. "I want to make a clock that chimes."

Benjamin began to work. He made a wonderful wooden clock. It chimed every hour. People came from all over America to see Benjamin's wonderful clock.

Benjamin also liked to read books about the sun, moon, and stars. He learned so much about the sun, moon, and stars that he wrote a book about them. The book was called an almanac. It told of many things that happened in the sky.

Benjamin Banneker became so well known that President George Washington chose him to help plan the city of Washington, D.C.

KNOWING BENJAMIN BANNEKER

Can you imagine a little boy who enjoyed reading and studying more than he did playing with other children? This may seem difficult to imagine, but there really was such a boy. This boy, born on a farm near Baltimore, Maryland, grew to be a fine man. In fact, he achieved so much that he was later chosen by President George Washington to do a special job.

When Benjamin Banneker was very young, his grandmother taught him to read. When the time came for him to start school, he was far ahead of most of the other children. His favorite subject was arithmetic.

At the age of fifteen, Benjamin had finished school. He wanted to go to college and learn more. However, Benjamin's parents did not have the money to pay for his college. Benjamin was not to be stopped because of that. He began reading everything he could find. He would look for the hardest arithmetic problems, just for the fun of trying to solve them. Sometimes he even made up very difficult problems for himself. Benjamin soon began receiving letters from people from different parts of the country asking him to solve their problems.

One day, Benjamin borrowed a watch from a friend. He wanted to study it to see how it worked. After studying the watch for a long time, he began to work. When he finished, he had made a wonderful wooden clock that kept very good time. It has been said that this clock was the first made in America that could strike on the hour. People from all over the country heard about Benjamin's wonderful clock and came to see it.

In later years, Benjamin found a friend who had a

huge library of books. Benjamin's friend said Benjamin could borrow and read as many books as he liked. Many of the books Benjamin read were about the sun, the moon, and the stars. He became so interested that he began to study about the sun, moon, stars, and other heavenly bodies. This study is called astronomy. Benjamin learned so much that he wrote an almanac. An almanac is a book that tells of things that happen in the sky. He also wrote what he thought the weather would be for many months to come.

Benjamin Banneker became so well known for his accomplishments that he was chosen by President Washington to help plan the city of Washington, D.C.

UNDERSTANDING BENJAMIN BANNEKER

Benjamin Banneker was born November 9, 1731, near Baltimore, Maryland. His father was a slave but his mother was free. They instilled in their son the idea of studying and had high hopes for him to make a success in the world. Benjamin did not disappoint his parents. He studied very hard and was sent to a private school near Baltimore. At school, Benjamin distinguished himself with his work in mathematics.

The nearest neighbors to the Bannekers were a Quaker family named Ellicott. Their son, George, became interested and friendly with Benjamin when he had finished school. The Ellicotts owned a large library with many books. The family loaned Benjamin many books and encouraged him to read. They also encouraged him to study mathematics and astronomy. Benjamin became very interested in both these subjects. He wanted to study and learn as much as possible. He was to study and learn for many years.

Benjamin had a very inquiring mind. One day he borrowed his friend George's watch. Benjamin wanted to study the watch. He wanted to see what made it work. He studied the watch for several days. Then be began working. He made a large wooden clock that actually kept time. Moreover, the clock would strike every hour on the hour. People around Baltimore heard about the clock and came to see it. They told their friends and soon visitors came from many places to see the wonderful clock.

Benjamin continued to study at the Ellicott home. He became more interested in making mathematical calculations relating to the stars and constellations. Moreover, he was able to predict solar eclipses and other phenomena about the heavens from his calculations based on older astronomical information. He had found the tables in one of the Ellicott's many books.

Benjamin continued his mathematical calculations. His predictions were so accurate that he was consulted by his neighbors. He was also consulted by strangers. He was so accurate that he even found mistakes in the calculations of some of the leading authorities of his day!

In 1792, Benjamin finally prepared his own almanac and had it published. The almanac was published by a Baltimore publishing company. Benjamin was 61 years old when his almanac was published.

The almanac included time of eclipses, hours of sunrise, hours of sunset, and tide tables for Chesapeake Bay and nearby waters. It also included weather predictions for festival days, holidays, and days for holding Circuit Court.

There were very few newspapers in the area at this time, and thus, the almanac filled a great need.

Benjamin sent a copy of his almanac to Thomas Jefferson. Thomas Jefferson was the Secretary of State in President George Washington's Cabinet. Thomas Jefferson liked the almanac and sent it on to the Academy of Science in Paris, France. The almanac was praised by the Academy. This was a great honor for Benjamin.

George Ellicott, Benjamin's lifelong friend, had become a member of the Commission that was to plan the city of Washington, D.C. George Ellicott recommended that Benjamin also serve on this Commission. Ellicott made the recommendation to Thomas Jefferson. Jefferson suggested Benjamin Banneker's name to President Washington. Thus, the President appointed Benjamin to the commission.

There was a great deal of confusion within the Commission. Major L'Enfant received very little cooperation from some of the American engineers working on the Commission. He quit and returned to France. However,

Benjamin had seen the plans and he was able to reproduce them. Washington, D.C., the seat of the United States government and the home of our President, is indeed a beautiful city thanks to Benjamin Banneker.

REMEMBERING BENJAMIN BANNEKER

A. KNOWING YOUR VOCABULARY

almanac, 7 astronomy, 9
accomplishments, 9 constellations, 10

B. THINGS TO REMEMBER

1. Where was Benjamin Banneker born?
2. What did he make by himself?
3. What was the title of the book he wrote?
4. What was the subject of the book he wrote?
5. What was the name of the city he helped plan?

C. THINGS TO THINK AND TALK ABOUT

1. Benjamin Banneker said he liked to read more than he liked to play. Some people think reading is fun. Some people do not. Do you think reading is fun? Why? Why not?
2. Benjamin Banneker made a clock. Have you ever made anything? Have you ever thought of making something? What have you made or what would you like to make?
3. Benjamin Banneker was interested in the science of astronomy. Is there any area of science in which you are interested? What?
4. Benjamin Banneker wrote an almanac. How does an almanac differ from other books? What subjects would you need to learn before writing an almanac?

5. Benjamin Banneker helped to design the plans for the city of Washington, D.C. What would be your feelings or thoughts if you were visiting Washington?

D. THINGS TO DO

1. Benjamin Banneker studied the sky. Make a 'shape' book that corresponds with an astronomical body or atmospheric mass. (stars, clouds, sun, crescent moon, etc.)
2. Discuss the work involved in planning a city. Lay out the plans for a model city on a table or in a sand box using various materials.

E. BIBLIOGRAPHY

Adams, Russell. *Great Negroes Past and Present*. Afro-American Company, 1964.

Hughes, Langston and Meltzer, Milton. *A Pictorial History of the Negro In America*. Crown, 1963.

Patrick, John J. *The Progress of the Afro-American*. Benefic Press, 1968. For use at Junior High level.

Rollins, Charlemae. *They Showed the Way*. Crowell, 1964.

FREDERICK DOUGLASS
(1817 - 1895)
Fighter for Freedom

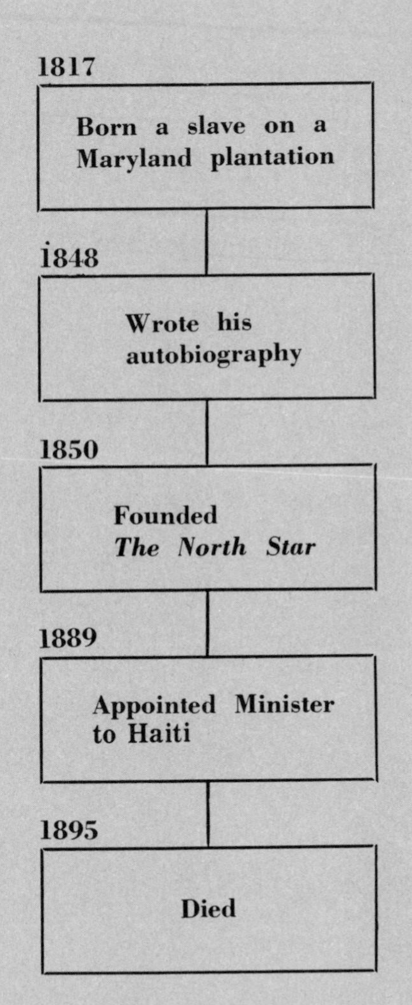

We look to mixed schools to teach that worth and ability are to be the criterion of manhood and not race and color.

Frederick Douglass
Abolition Speech

MEETING FREDERICK DOUGLASS

Frederick was a slave who worked for young master Tommy Auld in Baltimore, Maryland. Every day Tommy's mother gave him reading and writing lessons. Fred liked to sit and listen to the lessons. One day, Tommy's mother said, "Fred, would you like to learn the ABC's, too?"

"Yes, Mrs. Auld, I would like to learn."

Fred joined Tommy at his lessons with Mrs. Auld. When Tommy's father found out about the lessons, he was very angry. "You will have to stop teaching Fred," he said. "It is not good for slaves to learn to read and write because they will want to be free."

Fred had to buy a book and continue learning by himself. When he had learned to read and write, he began to teach other slaves to read and write. After Fred became free, he made speeches against slavery. He did much to help slaves become free men.

KNOWING FREDERICK DOUGLASS

Frederick Douglass was born in the backwoods of Maryland. When he was very young, he was taken from his home and sent to live with an old woman on another plantation. The old woman was very cruel.

When Frederick was five years old, he was sent to the home of his master's brother in Baltimore. His job was errand boy and servant. When the master's son received his lessons, Fred would sit and listen. He began to learn to read. At night, Fred learned to write in secret. He bought a book for fifty cents and he would copy words from the book.

When Fred was sixteen, he was sent back to the plantation in Maryland. Fred usually went to church every Sunday. He was asked to teach Sunday School because he could read and write. Fred was glad to help. He thought that by teaching other slaves to read he might help them attain their freedom. The slave owners did not want their slaves to learn to read. They were very angry. Fred's master was so mad that he sent him to another plantation for punishment. The master at this plantation was very cruel and often beat Fred.

After a year, Fred was sent to another plantation. The master was kind and allowed Fred to start his Sunday School Class again. Fred planned to escape but was discovered and sent to Baltimore once more.

He obtained a job building ships. He made friends with a sailor named Benny. Benny took Fred to a meeting of Negro people.

Fred escaped from slavery by borrowing Benny's sailor suit and his papers.

Fred began to think of the many people who were slaves but who wanted freedom. He began speaking against slavery and became a popular speaker. He also wrote his autobiography—the story of his life.

His old master read the autobiography and sent men to bring Frederick back to him. Fred escaped and went to England for a year. He was very popular because of his autobiography and because he was such a good speaker. Fred's friends bought the papers from his master. Fred became a free man.

He returned to the United States and with Anna and his family moved to Rochester, New York. He began publishing his own newspaper, *The North Star*.

Thus, because of his fight against slavery, Frederick became an honored person in the United States and in the rest of the world.

UNDERSTANDING FREDERICK DOUGLASS

Frederick Douglass was born in the backwoods of Maryland in the year, 1817. When he was born, he was not called Frederick Douglass, but was named Fred Bailey.

When Fred was eleven, he bought himself a copy of *The Columbian Orator* for fifty cents.

Fred wanted to learn how to write. At night, he would secretly copy words from the Bible and *The Columbian Orator*. If there was no one at home, he would go into the library and use the pen and the ink at his master's desk, and thus slowly learned to write. Fred remained in Baltimore until he was about thirteen, but then his master died and Fred was returned to the plantation so that he could be sent elsewhere. Fred was lucky because he was sent back to Baltimore to work for the Hugh Aulds until he was sixteen. However, Master Thomas and Master Hugh had an argument, and Fred was sent back to Maryland. The plantation was located at the oyster-fishing village of St. Michaelson on the Miles River. Master Thomas' plantation was run by an overseer.

On one occasion, Fred was teaching a large group of slaves their ABC's when a group of slave owners entered the Sunday School classroom. The slave owners were angry. They did not want their slaves to be taught to read and write. They thought that if the slave was educated, he then might want to be free.

Master Thomas, Fred's master, was very angry. He said, "So that's what you learned in Baltimore. Well, I'm glad I found out before it went too far! I know the medicine for you!

Before anything would happen to Fred, he boarded a train leaving for Philadelphia, Pennsylvania. He had his friend, Benny's sailor suit and papers on. Fred proudly showed the papers he had borrowed from Benny to the conductor. The conductor then sold Fred a ticket to Philadelphia. Fred arrived safely and then took a train to New York City. He also hoped to free his friend Anna.

Fred wrote Anna. She came to New York within a week and on the day she arrived they were married. A few days later they were on their way to New Bedford, Massachusetts. When the young couple arrived in New Bedford, they went to the home of Mr. and Mrs. Nathan Johnson, a friend of David Ruggles. They told the Johnsons their story. The Johnsons took the young couple into their home.

During the first evening, while talking to Mr. Johnson, Fred explained that he couldn't keep the name of Bailey because his owner might be looking for him. Mr. Johnson suggested the name of Douglass because he had been reading a story about a man named Douglass when the young couple had knocked at the door. Frederick liked the new name and from then on he always used the name Frederick Douglass.

Fred found a job in a factory. When he got his first wages, he rented a house for Anna and himself.

Two years later, a very important speaker, William Lloyd Garrison, came to town to give a lecture. After the talk, Frederick asked him many questions and gave his views on the subject of slavery. When he returned to New York, Mr. Garrison was interviewed by a reporter about his lecture trip. He made mention of Frederick Douglass as a very intelligent young man. It was reported in the newspaper and Frederick was very proud.

In the summer of 1841, Frederick and a group of friends went to Nantucket to hear Mr. Garrison speak again. Mr. Garrison remembered Frederick and when he was finished speaking he asked Frederick to tell what it was like to be a slave. Frederick was nervous but he spoke very well.

The next day, the members of the Massachusetts Anti-Slavery Society asked him to become a member. He joined the Society and became one of their main speakers. Frederick went from town to town and city to city attempting to tell everyone about what it was like to be a slave. He became a very popular speaker. Frederick also took time to write a book, *The Narrative Of Frederick Douglass*. In the book, he told about belonging to Mr. Thomas Auld. Mr. Thomas Auld read the book and went to court to demand the return of his slave, Frederick Douglass. Frederick heard about Mr. Auld's action and immediately decided to leave the United States. He went to Boston and sailed on a steamship for London, just three hours before agents came to get him.

Frederick travelled in Ireland, Scotland, and England for a year. He was well-known because of his book and because he had escaped from his master for a second time. Frederick spoke to large groups throughout the three countries. The week before he was to leave London, the British Anti-Slavery Society held a large banquet for him. At the banquet they presented him with the papers that proved he was a free man. They had purchased his freedom from Mr. Thomas Auld. Frederick came back to the United States a free man and with a desire to start his own newspaper. He and his family moved to Rochester, New York, and started a newspaper called, *The North Star*. *The North Star* was published weekly and was read by many people. Frederick Douglass was considered an authority on the Afro-American point of view regarding slavery.

When the Civil War broke out, Abraham Lincoln sent for Frederick Douglass. Abraham Lincoln and Frederick became friends. Frederick continued publishing his newspaper in Rochester until the Emancipation Proclamation was issued. This proclamation marked the end of slavery in the United States.

In 1877, Frederick was appointed a Marshal of the District of Columbia. Frederick's duties were not too important but it left him free to continue to make speeches and write newspaper articles. In 1881, Frederick became the Recorder of Deeds for the District.

In 1889, Frederick was appointed to the post of Minister to Haiti.

Frederick Douglass died in 1895. He was an honored person in the United States and the world because of his fight for freedom.

REMEMBERING FREDERICK DOUGLASS

A. KNOWING YOUR VOCABULARY

plantation, 16 autobiography, 17
Emancipation Proclamation, 21

B. THINGS TO REMEMBER

1. Why was Fred sent to the slave breaker?
2. Where did Fred work after he returned to Baltimore?
3. What was the name of the newspaper edited by Frederick Douglass?
4. Who was the President who became Fred's friend?
5. When did Frederick Douglass die?

C. THINGS TO TALK AND THINK ABOUT

1. Slaves were not permitted to read. How do you think Fred felt when Mrs. Auld offered to teach him how to read? How did you feel when you read the first time?
2. Why did Mr. Auld become angry when he found out that Fred was learning to read? How would you feel if someone stopped you from reading? What would you do?
3. Fred delivered many speeches against slavery. What is a speech? Have you ever heard a speech? What was the speech about?
4. Fred taught reading and writing to other slaves. Have you ever thought of becoming a teacher? Why? Why not?
5. After Fred returned to Baltimore, he and Benny became friends. Benny helped Fred in his fight for freedom. Have you ever received help from a friend? When? Have you ever given help to a friend? How?

D. THINGS TO DO

1. Make an ABC book of words or phrases for Frederick Douglass and the period in which he lived. e.g. A - Anna, Auld
   B - Baltimore, Benny
   S - shipyard, slave
   T - ticket, trade
   U - Underground Railroad
2. Assemble a chart listing the ways children today could earn money to buy their own books.

E. BIBLIOGRAPHY

Bontemps, Arna. *Frederick Douglass: Slave-Fighter-Freeman*. Alfred A. Knopf, 1959.

Douglass, Frederick. (Edited by Benjamin Quorles) *Narrative of The Life of Frederick Douglass*. Belleknapp Press. 1960.

Patterson, Lillie. *Frederick Douglass, Freedom Fighter*. Garrard. 1965.

Ritchie, Barbara. *The Mind And Heart of Frederick Douglass: Excerpts From Speeches of the Great Negro Orator*. Crowell. 1968.

Stratton, Madeline Robinson. *Negroes Who Helped Build America*. Ginn & Co. 1965.

HARRIET TUBMAN
(1820 - 1913)
Led over 300 Slaves to Freedom

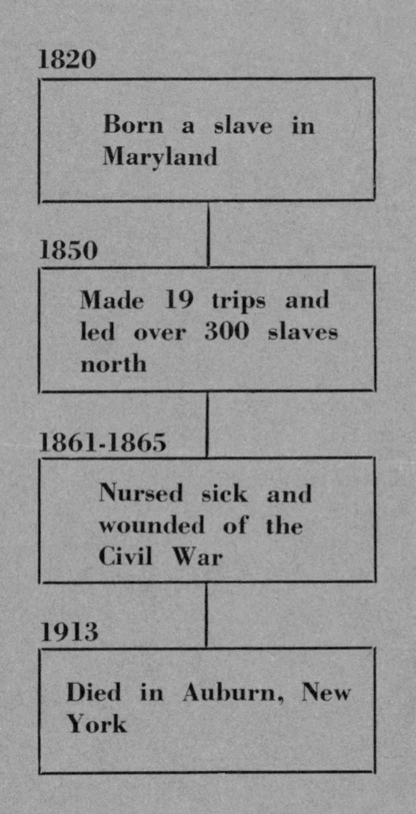

I have had the applause of the crowd and the satisfaction that comes of being approved by the multitude, while the most that you have done has been witnessed by a few trembling, scarred, and foot sore bondmen and women, whom you have led out of the house of bondage, and whose heartfelt "God bless you" has been your only reward.

Frederick Douglass
Letter to Harriet Tubman

MEETING HARRIET TUBMAN

Harriet Tubman was working in the field.
She was a slave.
She worked hard.
A little boy walked in the field.
He walked near Harriet so she could hear him.
"Harriet, the master is going to sell you." he whispered.
Her heart beat fast.
"I know what I must do," she thought.
Harriet ran to her cabin.
She put food and a knife into her bag.
Harriet could not say goodbye to anyone, not even to her mother and father.
Her escape had to be very secret.
The night was dark and cold.
The woods were dark and scary.
"I will follow the North Star," she said.
"I must go on!" she thought.
Hunting dogs followed her.
Harriet heard the dogs barking.
"They are on my trail.
I must lose them."
Harriet was walking beside a muddy river.
She slid quickly into the deep water.
"The dogs will lose my trail
when they reach the river bank."
Harriet stayed in the cold river for many hours.
She waded through water for many miles.

Finally, she climbed the river bank, hungry and tired.
Suddenly the sound of horses' hoofs broke the stillness.
"I must hide until they pass," thought Harriet.
She jumped into the ditch just in time.
The riders drew near and tied up their horses.
The men made a fire and cooked their food.
Harriet looked through the bushes and saw five men.
"I am going to be free," promised Harriet to herself.
"I will never let them find me."
The slave catchers never caught her.
Harriet walked many nights.
She hid many days.
She followed the shining star to freedom.
She found the North.
She found friends in the North.
She found freedom in the North.
Harriet Tubman dreamed a dream long ago—
"I'm going to be free. I'm going to be free."
Harriet Tubman's dream came true.

Do you have a dream that *YOU* hope comes true???

KNOWING HARRIET TUBMAN

Harriet Tubman was born in a small cabin on a plantation in Maryland. She was working in the fields by the time she was eight years old. She also had to work in the master's big house as well as in the fields. Harriet's main job was to watch the master's baby. If the baby cried, Harriet was often whipped.

One day, when Harriet was thirteen years old, a slave on the plantation ran away. The slave ran to the village store. Harriet followed him to see what was going to happen. The slave-catcher picked up a heavy iron weight from the storekeeper's scales. He threw it at the slave who was running away. The heavy iron weight hit Harriet instead of the run-away slave. She fell to the ground. Harriet was sick for a very long time. She never got completely well. She had a bad scar where the iron weight had hit her. Harriet also had strange sleeping spells. She never knew when or where she might go to sleep.

When Harriet recovered, she was sent to another plantation to work. At this plantation she met John Tubman. John was a free Negro, not a slave. Moreover, he was paid for working in the fields. John Tubman and Harriet were married.

All her life Harriet had dreamed of freedom. Now that she was married to a free man she wanted to be free more than ever. Harriet wanted to escape to the North. She knew that there were people along the way who would hide runaway slaves and help them to get their freedom.

When it was time to escape, Harriet begged her husband to go with her. He would not go. Two of Harriet's brothers said they would go with her. Harriet and her brothers left the plantation in the middle of the night. After a while her brothers became scared and decided to turn back. They dragged Harriet back with them.

A few days later Harriet decided to try to escape by herself. Harriet felt freedom was worth the danger. Harriet went to a farmer for help. He was a conductor on the Underground Railroad. He put a sack over her and drove her in his wagon to the next station. From station to station, Harriet traveled by night, walking and hiding, until she finally reached the state of Pennsylvania. At last she was free.

She, too, became a conductor on the Underground Railroad and helped many slaves reach freedom. Harriet led so many slaves to freedom that she was called "Moses" by her people.

UNDERSTANDING HARRIET TUBMAN

When Harriet was about thirteen, she was sent to work in the fields. On one occasion a slave ran away from the plantation. Harriet followed him to the village store. The overseer wanted Harriet to stop the slave. She refused and the slave ran from the store. The overseer picked up a two-pound metal weight from the storekeeper's scale. He threw it at the slave but missed him. The weight struck Harriet in the forehead and she fell to the ground. She was near death and remained unconscious for days. Harriet recovered but there was a deep scar where the iron weight had struck. For the rest of her life, she had strange sleeping spells. Harriet never knew when or where she would fall asleep.

After recovering from the blow, Harriet was sent to work for another master. A few years later she met John Tubman. He was a free Negro. When he worked, he was paid for the job. They were married soon after they met. Harriet was happy now, except for one thing. She wanted to be free. She had heard about some slaves who were escaping with the help of the Underground Railroad. The Underground Railroad was a series of roads and paths that led to the North. The stations on the Underground Railroad were homes of people who would hide runaway slaves and help them on the way. The conductors on the Underground Railroad were Quakers, free Afro-Americans, and others who came secretly to the South to lead groups of slaves to freedom. The only ticket one needed was to be a slave who wanted freedom. They usually followed the North Star to freedom.

Harriet went to a farmer for help. He was a conductor

on the Underground Railroad. He put a sack over her and drove her in his wagon to the next station. From station to station Harriet traveled by night, walking and hiding, until she finally reached Pennsylvania. At last she was free.

While in Philadelphia, Harriet met William Sill, a free Negro and a conductor on the Underground Railroad. Harriet familiarized herself with the workings of the railroad. Moreover, she saved much of the money that she earned while working as a servant. With her savings and new knowledge, Harriet prepared to go South so that she might help members of her family reach freedom. In December of 1850, Harriet made her first trip as a conductor on the Underground Railroad. She led her sister's family to freedom.

Harriet helped many more slaves to escape to freedom. However, it gradually became more difficult to help slaves find the road to freedom, because of the Fugitive Slave Law of 1850. This law held that any runaway slave must be sent back to his Southern master. Harriet also had many narrow and exciting escapes while conducting slaves to freedom. Nevertheless, she helped over 300 slaves reach the North.

On one occasion, Harriet was in a railroad station. She overheard a conversation between two men regarding a forty thousand dollar reward—for the capture of Harriet Tubman. These men spotted the black woman sitting in the station and became suspicious. Quick thinking again helped to remove Harriet from a dangerous situation. Although she couldn't read, Harriet quickly picked up the newspaper on the bench next to her and pretended to be reading from it. The suspicion was removed when one of the men said, "That can't be Harriet Tubman. She can't read or write."

"Female Moses", as Harriet came to be called, planned her freedom campaigns like a military chief of staff. She enforced ironclad discipline on the trips. She revealed few of her plans to anyone. However, her people trusted her implicitly.

Escape to freedom became more hazardous and difficult with each trip. The Fugitive Slave Law further hampered the freedom express, thereby making it necessary for Harriet to extend the Underground Railroad to Canada. One of the stations was Rochester, New York. There, Frederick Douglass, Susan B. Anthony, and other abolitionists opened their homes to assist runaway slaves. Usually, Rochester was the last stop before going to Canada. From 1851 to 1857, Harriet made St. Catharines in Canada her base. She made eleven raids on Maryland and neighboring states from here.

Six years after she had left home, Harriet returned for her parents. They were very old and unable to walk very far. Harriet got a wagon and secretly drove them to a railroad. They were over 70 years old when they made their freedom escape with Harriet.

She used to say proudly, "On my Underground Railroad, I never ran my train off the track and I never lost a passenger."

It was during the war that Harriet's sincere interest in humanity had another opportunity to prove itself. She nursed many soldiers back to health. Skin color made no difference to Harriet. She made medicines from plants and roots and cured many men who needed aid.

She also became a spy for the Union Army and helped soldiers to rescue many slaves from southern plantations. In July, 1863, Harriet became the leader of a party of scouts and river pilots who spied on the enemy and turned in some valuable information which helped to save the lives of many soldiers.

In 1869 she returned to live in Auburn, New York. She took care of the sick and poor in her own home and lived to be more than 93 years old. She died in Auburn, New York, in 1913.

People all over the land will never forget her.

REMEMBERING HARRIET TUBMAN

A. KNOWING YOUR VOCABULARY

conductor, 28   Underground Railroad, 28

B. THINGS TO REMEMBER

1. What is meant by the *Underground Railroad*?
2. Which law made it more difficult for people to help slaves escape to the North?
3. What dangers did Harriet encounter as a conductor with the Underground Railroad?
4. What special name was given to Harriet?
5. How did Harriet contribute to our nation's history?

C. THINGS TO THINK AND TALK ABOUT

1. Harriet Tubman escaped to freedom. She had to keep her escape a secret. Have you ever kept a secret? Was it easy? Was it hard? Why?
2. Harriet traveled at night. She was often frightened. Have you ever been frightened? What scared you?
3. Harriet was a slave on the plantation. She took care of young children. Have you ever cared for younger children?
4. Because Harriet helped many slaves to freedom, she endangered her own life. Have you ever helped anyone even when you might have been hurt while helping? Have you ever helped a friend? Has any friend ever helped you? What makes a person a 'friend'?
5. Harriet made her home in the city of Auburn, New York. If you moved to another city, state or country, where would you choose to live? Why?
6. Harriet's dream of freedom was realized. Do you

have a wish or a dream? What are your wishes? How will you make your dreams come true?

D. THINGS TO DO

1. Write a biography on the life of Harriet Tubman.
2. Make a picture book for the school library, illustrating events in Harriet's life described by the children in their class biography.

E. BIBLIOGRAPHY

Bradford, Sarah. *Harriet Tubman: The Moses of Her People*. Corinth Press. 1961.

Dolin, Arnold. *Great American Heroines*. Hart Publishing Co. 1960.

Humphreville, Francis T. *Harriet Tubman*. Houghton Mifflin. 1967.

McGovern, Ann. *Runaway Slave: The Story of Harriet Tubman*. Four Winds Press. 1965.

Petry, Ann Lane. *Harriet Tubman, Conductor On The Underground Railroad*. Crowell. 1955.

JAN E. MATZELIGER
(1852 - 1889)
Inventor of the Shoe Last Machine

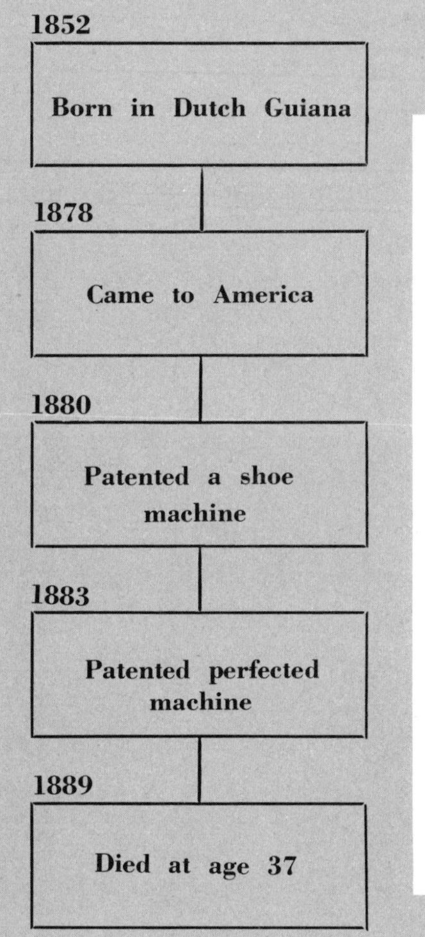

Can we as a nation continue together permanently - forever - half slave, and half free? The problem is too mighty for me.

Abraham Lincoln
Speech about Slavery

MEETING JAN E. MATZELIGER

Black shoes! Brown shoes! Red shoes! White shoes! You can see many colors of shoes if you look around.

Jan was a worker. He worked for his father. He worked on machines. Jan liked machines.

Jan wanted to work in America. He wanted to save money. He wanted to become rich. Jan came to America.

He went to work. He made shoes. He was called a cobbler. Cobblers are people who make shoes. Making shoes was very slow work.

Jan said, "I will make a machine—a machine to make shoes."

Some of the workers said, "You can't do that. No one can do that."

Jan thought and thought. He took little boxes and other things. He put them together. He made a little machine. Soon he made a big machine that was like the little machine. The big machine worked. It made a shoe all by itself. Jan was very happy. All the cobblers were happy. Now they could make many shoes.

One day a big company bought his machine. Even today, this company makes machines. They sell the machine. The machines make many, many shoes.

Jan was an inventor. He made something useful. Would you like to invent something? Think hard and maybe you can.

KNOWING JAN E. MATZELIGER

Jan Matzeliger was born September 15, 1852 in Dutch Guiana. Jan liked working with machines.

Jan knew that there was no machine that could make shoes. Most shoes were made by hand. Many shoemakers, working all day, made only about 6 pairs of shoes.

On March 20, 1883, Jan finished and patented his machine. Jan Matzeliger's shoe machine could do many things. It could arrange the leather over the sole of the shoe. It could sew the leather together and drive 350 nails in one minute. Shoemakers could make 1000 pairs of shoes in one day using Jan's machine.

Jan's machines were used in many shoe factories. They are still used today.

UNDERSTANDING
JAN E. MATZELIGER

For many years shoes had to be made by hand. This was very hard work and took a very long time. Because so much work was put into making a pair of shoes, the price for them was often very high. The shoemakers wished very much for a machine that could make shoes, but no one knew how to make such a machine. Many men attempted to make such a machine but no one succeeded.

Jan Matzeliger was born September 15, 1852, in Paramberio, Dutch Guiana, in South America. When he was old enough he worked in his father's machine shop. He enjoyed operating the machines. He was fascinated by the way they worked and the things they did. In 1878, Jan and his family moved to Lynn, Massachusetts, in the United States. For many years, he worked as a shoemaker's apprentice at the Harney Brothers' Factory learning to make shoes.

One day while he was in the factory he heard a workman say, "No man can ever build a machine that will last shoes." "Last" means to shape or form.

Jan believed he could build a machine that could make shoes. He worked on his plans and built a model of this machine. However, he was still not satisfied with it. He questioned the workmen and watched the motions of the men's hands. The men's hands would grip the leather and sew it at the same time.

Jan felt there must be a way to improve his machine. He worked four more years and in September, 1880, he had a machine that pleated the leather around the toe and heel of a shoe. Jan was offered $1,500 for his machine, but he refused to sell it because it could not do all the things he wanted the machine to do. Jan continued to work on his machine for a few more years until it was perfect. At last he had done it! On March 20, 1883, he patented his machine. A patent is a license given by the government so no one will try to steal or copy an invention.

Jan Matzeliger's shoe machine could arrange the leather over the sole of the shoe. It could sew the leather together and drive 350 nails in one minute. Using the old method a large number of shoemakers could only make about 60 pairs of shoes a day. However, the same number of men, using Jan's machine, could make about 1,000 pairs in a day.

Many shoe factories began to use Jan's machinery. A large company purchased Jan's invention. Gradually, shoes became cheaper. Thus, many people were happy over the Matzeliger shoe-making machine.

Jan worked long and hard and had neglected his health. He developed tuberculosis and died on August 24, 1889, at the age of 37. He willed all of his shoe-machine stock to his church. In 1904 the church was able to pay off its mortgage thanks to Jan E. Matzeliger.

A fitting tribute was paid to Jan Ernest Matzeliger in the December, 1918 article in the *The Three Partners*. The magazine is published by the United Shoe Machinery Corporation in Boston, Massachusetts. The article said, in part, "As Elias Howe was to the sewing machine, so was Jan Matzeliger to the shoe-lasting machine. They both did the impossible."

REMEMBERING JAN E. MATZELIGER

A. KNOWING YOUR VOCABULARY

cobbler, 35 patent, 38

B. THINGS TO REMEMBER

1. When was Jan Matzeliger born?

2. Why did Jan come to America?
3. What was Jan's first job in America?
4. Where did Jan live in the United States?
5. Why did Jan refuse to sell his machine?

C. THINGS TO THINK AND TALK ABOUT

1. Jan saved money so he could come to America. If you needed money for something important, how would you go about getting it?
2. Have you ever used any machines? Make a list of machines you have used.
3. Jan invented a machine to make shoes. Have you ever thought of inventing a machine? What would your machine do that no other machine can do?

D. THINGS TO DO

1. Make individual storybooks illustrating important events in the life of Jan Matzeliger.
2. Locate Jan's birthplace on a map and trace his journey to Lynn, Massachusetts.

E. BIBLIOGRAPHY

Rollins, Charlemae. *They Showed the Way*. Crowell. 1964.

Spangler, Earl. *The Negro in America*. Lerner Publication Company. 1967.

BOOKER T. WASHINGTON
(1858 - 1915)
Educator
Founder of Tuskegee Institute

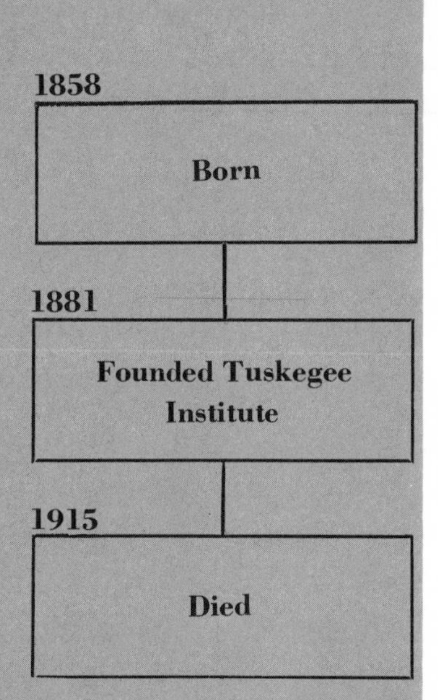

No race can prosper till it learns that there is as much dignity in tilling a field as in writing a poem. It is at the bottom of life we must begin, and not at the top. Nor should we permit our grievances to overshadow our opportunities.

Booker T. Washington

MEETING BOOKER T. WASHINGTON

Booker T. Washington was born on a slave plantation. When Booker and his mother were freed, they went to join Booker's stepfather in Malden, West Virginia.

Booker had to work in the salt mines because his family needed money. Booker went to school at night and worked in the salt mines during the day. Booker did not stay in school very long. He went to work in the coal mines. From the men in the coal mines he heard about a school called Hampton Institute.

When he had saved enough money, he left his home to go away to school. When he ran out of money, he worked on a ship during the day. At night, he usually slept under a wooden sidewalk. When he reached Hampton, he went to the office and asked if he could become a student. The principal at the school said yes. Booker was very happy.

When Booker finished school, he became a teacher. Soon he opened a school of his own. It was called Tuskegee Institute. Tuskegee Institute is a very famous school in the South.

KNOWING BOOKER T. WASHINGTON

Booker T. Washington was born a slave on a southern plantation about 1858. After the Civil War, Booker and his mother were freed. They went to join Booker's stepfather in Malden, West Virginia. Booker began working in the salt mines with his stepfather.

At night Booker and his mother tried to learn the alphabet. They used an old spelling book that his mother had found.

One day, a man came to Malden who could read and write. All the Negro people put thier money together to pay the man to open a school so they could learn to read. However, Booker could not go to school during the day. He had to work in the salt mines because his family needed the money he earned.

Booker went to school at night. He was a very good student. His mother worked out a plan so Booker could go to school during the day. He went to work at the salt mines at four o'clock every morning. He worked until it was time to go to school. He went to school all day, then went back to work in the salt mines until late at night.

Booker did not stay in school very long. He was getting older and could work in the coal mines where he earned more money. While working in the coal mines, he heard about a school in Virginia called Hampton Institute. He wanted to go to Hampton Institute. He began to save his money and when he thought he had enough money, he left home to go away to school.

Booker traveled by stagecoach to Richmond, Virginia. He ran out of money so he worked on ships during the day and usually slept under a wooden sidewalk at night.

When he had enough money he went to Hampton and asked to be a student at the school. The school admitted him.

When he finished his schooling, he returned to Malden, West Virginia, and became a teacher. He was such a good teacher that he was invited to return to Hampton to teach.

In 1881, Booker went to Tuskegee, Alabama, to open a school. The school grew from one old building with 30 students to many fine buildings with many students.

Tuskegee Institute became the most famous vocational school in the South. Booker T. Washington was the President of Tuskegee, until his death in 1915.

UNDERSTANDING BOOKER T. WASHINGTON

Booker T. Washington was born in a slave plantation cookhouse about 1858. His mother was the plantation cook and he and his mother lived in the cookhouse. Because the fireplace was always burning, it was usually a very hot place in the summer and a very smokey place in the winter.

After the Civil War, Booker and his mother were freed and they joined Booker's stepfather in Malden, West Virginia. Booker went to work in the salt mines with his stepfather. Booker and his mother tried to learn the alphabet at night. They used an old spelling book that his mother had found.

Then with his mother's help, Booker started going to night classes.

The first day that Booker went to school was an exciting time for him. He was going to learn to read and write. The teacher began the day by asking each pupil his name so he could make a record of the class. As the teacher went from row to row recording names, Booker's heart began to beat very fast because every child in the class had two names, and some even had three names. When the teacher got to Booker and asked his name, he shouted out "Booker Washington". Booker never knew how the second name came to him but he liked the name and used it from then on. Later, he added a middle name, Taliaferro. It was a very hard name to pronounce. It was also a hard name to spell, he used only the initial for his middle name and most people called him Booker T. Washington.

From the salt mines, Booker went to work in the coal mines. The work in the coal mines was very dangerous.

It was here that Booker T. first heard about Hampton Institute in Virginia. At Hampton, a boy could work for an education. Booker T. decided that he wanted to go to Hampton.

Booker T. began to save his money. The people in town liked him so much that they gave him pennies, nickles, dimes, a handkerchief and a pair of socks to help him on his way. When Booker T. thought he had enough money, he left by stagecoach to go to Hampton. When the stagecoach stopped for the night, Booker T. was refused a room by the innkeeper. He walked up and down the road all night to try to keep warm until the stagecoach was ready to leave.

When the stagecoach arrived in Richmond, Booker T. had run out of money. He spent the night sleeping under a wooden sidewalk. When he awoke in the morning, he found that he was very near the river where a ship was unloading cargo. He asked for work and stayed in Richmond for several days. In order to save money, Booker T. continued to sleep under the wooden sidewalk almost every night.

As soon as he had saved enough money, he continued on his way to Hampton. He walked part of the way and arrived at school with fifty cents.

Booker T. was given a job as janitor at the school. He had to get up early to make the fires and then stay up late at night cleaning all the rooms, but he did receive an education. In 1875, Booker T. was graduated from Hampton with honors.

Booker T. returned to his home in Malden to become the town teacher. He also tutored several young men and helped them to enter Hampton. Booker T.'s young men were such good students that the President of Hampton invited him to return to Hampton to teach. Booker also had to supervise a dormitory of about 100 American Indians. He was a good supervisor and a good teacher.

In 1881, Booker T. was sent to Tuskegee, Alabama, to

establish a school. There were 30 students and their ages ranged from 15 to 40. The school was held in a run-down church with Booker T. Washington as the only teacher. There were no books and no equipment, but this was the beginning of Tuskegee Institute. The school grew from one run-down building to dozens of fine buildings; from one teacher to more than a hundred; from 30 students to 3,000; and, eventually, became the most famous vocational school in the country. As Tuskegee grew, so did the fame of Booker T. Washington.

Booker T. made many speeches, traveled a great deal, and received many honors. He was happiest, however, when he was at Tuskegee. He was the President of the school until his death in 1915.

REMEMBERING BOOKER T. WASHINGTON

A. KNOWING YOUR VOCABULARY

vocational school, 43 supervise, 46

B. THINGS TO REMEMBER

1. What boy was born on a slave plantation in 1858?
2. Where did Booker and his family live after they were free?
3. What was Booker's first job?
4. What was the name of the big school Booker wanted to attend?
5. What did Booker do after he graduated?

C. THINGS TO THINK AND TALK ABOUT

1. Booker T. Washington became a teacher. What would you like to be when you grow up?
2. Booker T. Washington was born a slave. How would you feel if you were a slave? Why would you want to be free? What would you do to es-

cape slavery?

3. Booker endured many hardships while saving money for school. If you were Booker, how would you earn money in order to pay for an education?
4. Booker worked very hard in the salt and coal mines. What is the hardest job that you ever had to do? Do you know someone who works hard at his job? Who? What is the job?
5. When Booker attended school for the first time, he adopted a last name for himself. Why do you think he chose the name of Washington? If you could change your name, how would you change it and why?

D. THINGS TO DO

1. Plan a mural depicting the important events in Booker T. Washington's life.
2. Write original stories about Booker T. Washington's life.
3. A postage stamp was designed in honor of Booker T. Washington. Design a stamp in honor of an Afro-American currently in the news and discuss why he should be honored.

E. BIBLIOGRAPHY

Denniston, Elinor. *Famous Makers of America*. Dodd, Mead. 1963.

Graham, Shirley. *Booker T. Washington: Educator of Hand, Head and Heart*. Messner. 1964.

Patterson, Lillie. *Booker T. Washington, Leader of his People*. Garrard. 1962.

DANIEL HALE WILLIAMS
(1858 - 1931)
Physician

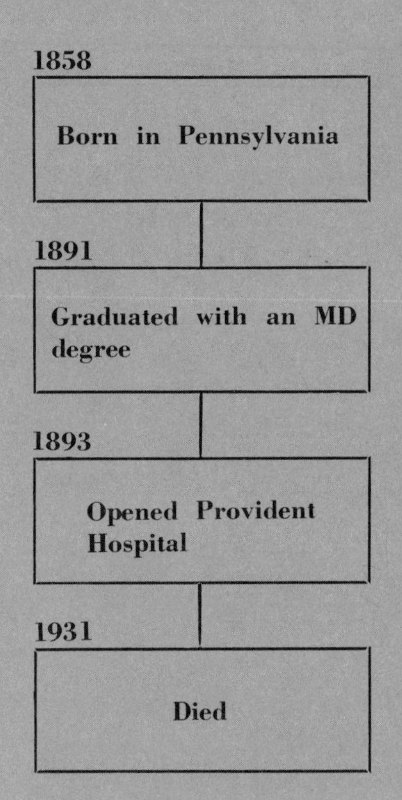

It is glorious - this history of ours!

Langston Hughes

MEETING DANIEL HALE WILLIAMS

It was raining outside. Dan Williams and his sister had to play inside.

"What do you want to be when you grow up?" Dorothy asked her brother Dan.

"I want to be a doctor," said Dan.

"Let's play hospital," said Dorothy. "You be the doctor. I'll be the nurse."

After they had played together for a long time, Dan said, "Maybe I'll be a real doctor someday. I like to help people."

When Dan grew up, that is just what happened. He worked hard to get the money to go to college to become a doctor.

Dr. Dan became a surgeon in a big hospital. A surgeon is a doctor who operates on people. One day a man came to the hospital. He was badly hurt. Dr. Dan operated on his heart and saved his life. Everyone was proud of Dr. Dan. The President of the United States asked him to come to Washington to teach other doctors what he had learned.

KNOWING DANIEL HALE WILLIAMS

Daniel Williams was born in Hollidaysville, Pennsylvania His father died when he was ten years old. His mother, his brother, and five sisters moved.

Daniel stayed in Pennsylvania to finish school. He missed his mother very much. He wanted to see her, but he had no money for a train ticket. A friendly ticket agent gave him a free pass and Daniel went to Wisconsin to join his family.

Daniel was very happy in Wisconsin, but when he was ready to go to school, he discovered he had left all of his books back in Pennsylvania. All he had was a dictionary. He learned many new words this way.

When Daniel finished school, he had no money to go to college. He worked as a shoemaker, as a barber, and in a law office. He dreamed of being a doctor. He worked very hard and finally saved enough money to enroll in medical school.

Dr. Dan became a surgeon at Provident Hospital in Chicago. One day a man was brought to the hospital with a bad stab wound in his heart. Everyone thought the man would die. Dr. Dan operated and sewed up the wound in the man's heart. This was the first time any one had operated successfully on the open heart.

President Grover Cleveland was so proud of Dr. Dan that he asked him to be the head of a hospital in Washington, D.C.

UNDERSTANDING DANIEL HALE WILLIAMS

Daniel Hale Williams was born in Hollidaysville, Pennsylvania, on January 18, 1858. Daniel's parents were free Negroes. He had a very happy childhood with his older brother and five sisters until he was about ten, when his father died. Daniel went to school every day and was a very good student.

After his father died, Daniel's mother moved the family to Janesville, Wisconsin, to live with relatives. Everyone went but Daniel. Daniel was left to stay with friends in Annapolis and to continue his schooling. He became very homesick and tried to board a train to take him to his family, but he had no money. A friendly ticket agent helped the young ten year old boy. He gave him a free railroad pass and Daniel travelled to Wisconsin to live with his family.

At the time Daniel went to school, most boys and girls only completed elementary school. Daniel worked so hard that he went on to what we know as high school. He went to Hare's Classical Academy and graduated from there. Since there was no money for Daniel to go to college, he went to work in a law office with the hope of becoming a lawyer. However, he did not really enjoy this kind of work and left it to try his hand at being a beginning shoemaker, a worker on a lake steamer, and a barber. He really wanted to be a doctor. He was helped in this desire by a barber friend who got him a job working in the office of the Surgeon General of the state of Wisconsin. He worked very hard. At the same time, he also studied. After two years he took the entrance examinations for the medical school at the Chicago Medical College. He passed the examinations and was graduated with his M.D. Degree in 1883. He then did his intern work at Mercy Hospital in Chicago, Illinois.

Most of this time, Dr. Dan Williams was also trying to help other Afro-American men and women who wanted to enter the medical profession. There were no schools where Negro girls could train for nursing, and there were no hopitals where Negro doctors could serve their internships. Dr. Dan Williams worked to organize and to establish Provident Hospital. Its doors were first opened in 1891. This was the first training school for Afro-American nurses in the United States.

Dr. Dan joined the staff of Provident Hospital as a surgeon. One day, he performed a major operation that was talked about everywhere. A man was brought to the emergency ward of the hospital with a bad stab wound. He was bleeding very much. Dr. Dan was called and examined the man. It was found that the man was still bleeding internally. Dr. Dan opened the wound and found that the man had been stabbed in the heart. There was a hole in the man's heart that was causing the bleeding. Everyone expected the man to die, but Dr. Dan decided to try to save him. Dr. Dan operated and sewed up the knife wound in the man's heart. Then he replaced the heart within its own walls while it continued beating. This operation required great skill, great daring, and a great doctor. The man lived. This was the first time this type of operation had ever been performed successfully. It was reported in all of the newspapers and medical journals.

In 1894, President Grover Cleveland called Dr. Dan to Washington and asked him to head the new Freeman's Hospital. Dr. Dan accepted the job and one of his first moves was to establish a nurses' training school in connection with the hospital.

In 1898, Dr. Dan resigned as head of Freemen's Hospital and returned to Chicago to enter private practice.

He continued to practice in Chicago at Cook County Hospital and also at St. Luke's Hospital until his death in 1931. He was elected a Fellow of the American College of Surgeons in 1913. This was a great honor to Dr. Daniel Hale Williams. He is regarded as one of America's greatest physicians.

REMEMBERING DR. DANIEL HALE WILLIAMS

A. KNOWING YOUR VOCABULARY

surgeon, 49 operated, 50 examinations, 52

B. THINGS TO REMEMBER

1. What boy lived to become a famous surgeon?
2. How old was Daniel when his father died?
3. What jobs did Daniel hold when he finished school?
4. Where did Daniel receive his medical training?
5. What were Daniel's contributions to our country's history?

C. THINGS TO THINK AND TALK ABOUT

1. When Dan Williams was a little boy, he liked to pretend he was a doctor. Do you ever pretend to be something? What? What other pretend games do you play?
2. Dan often played games with his sister. Who are your playmates? Who are your friends? Differentiate between the following words: friend, relative, playmate, pal, enemy. Draw a picture of your friends. Then draw a picture of yourself.
3. When Daniel's family moved, Dan had to stay in Pennsylvania. He missed his family? How would you feel?
4. Daniel forgot his books when he left Pennsylvania.

He had only his dictionary. If you could take only one book on a trip, which book would you choose?

5. Where were Daniel's contributions to our nation's history?

D. THINGS TO DO

1. Write a chart story of reasons why a doctor must excel in reading, arithmetic, spelling, etc.?
2. List items used by people in different professions or occupations.

stethoscope	baton	hammer
dolls	bat	pipes
pencil	hypodermic needle	scale
thermometer	suture	clock
books	scalpel	chisel

3. Write a newspaper account of Dr. Dan William's successful open heart surgery. Submit the finished article for publication in the school newspaper.

E. BIBLIOGRAPHY

Asimov, Isaac. *Break Throughs in Science*. Houghton, Mifflin Co. 1959

Buckler, Helen. *Dr. Dan: Pioneer American*. Little Brown & Co. 1954

Hughes, Langston. *Famous American Negroes*. Dodd, Mead. 1954.

HENRY OSSAWA TANNER
(1859 - 1937)
Master Painter in the Manner of the Renaissance

1859	Born
1880	Graduated from the Pennsylvania Academy of Fine Arts
1900	Won Lippincott Prize
1904	Won Louisiana Purchase Prize
1937	Died

We cannot neglect the great American contributors to American life.

John F. Kennedy

MEETING HENRY OSSAWA TANNER

One day, when Henry was 12 years old, he was playing ball in the park when he saw men painting a picture. Henry stopped playing ball to watch the men paint the picture. He watched the men paint for almost two hours. Then he ran home. With a pencil, he drew the same picture he had seen the men paint. From then on, Henry tried to draw everything he could find to draw.

His father and mother could not understand why Henry wanted to draw. They wanted him to be a minister like his father. Henry liked to go to church with his parents. He liked to hear his father preach. One day he told his father, "I wish I could talk to people like you do. Someday I'll make my pictures talk."

Henry's father, Bishop Tanner, was happy that his son liked his sermons. He was very happy when Henry said one day, "I'll paint your sermons when I get older."

For the rest of his life, that is what Henry did. He did not become a minister. He became a famous painter. He painted religious pictures. These pictures helped his father's sermons.

When Henry was older, Bishop Tanner said to him, "You are making your pictures talk to people just as you wished when you were a little boy."

KNOWING HENRY OSSAWA TANNER

Henry Tanner was born in Philadelphia, Pennsylvania. Henry's father was a minister. Henry's father hoped that his son would also become a minister.

One day, Henry went for a walk in a large park. He stopped to watch two men painting a sign. Henry watched the men paint the sign for almost two hours. When he left the park to go home, Henry knew he wanted to be a painter. He wanted to paint pictures like the two men in the park.

His mother and father had wanted Henry to be a minister, but they let him go to a school that taught painting. After he finished school, Henry did much painting. He also taught art at a college.

Henry wanted to go to Europe to study painting. He did not have enough money, so he collected all the pictures he had painted and had an "exhibit." An "exhibit" is a display of pictures that people can visit and purchase. Henry hoped to get enough money from his exhibit to travel to Europe. He did not sell one painting until the last day of the show. Then a minister and his wife bought most of Henry's paintings.

Henry went to Europe. When Henry got to Paris, France, he stopped his traveling in Europe. He had found a place where he could paint. He came home to visit for a short time, but Henry lived in Paris for the rest of his life.

Henry became famous for his religious paintings. He painted "Daniel in the Lion's Den" and "Christ Walking on the Water." He painted many other religious pictures.

A large museum is located one block from the spot where Henry Tanner decided to be a painter. In that museum is one of Henry's paintings. It is hanging in a place of honor today.

UNDERSTANDING
HENRY OSSAWA TANNER

Henry Tanner was born in Philadelphia in 1859. Henry's father was a minister in the African Episcopal Church. When Henry was born, his parents hoped that he would follow in his father's footsteps. When Henry's father became a bishop, their dreams increased.

Henry was walking in Fairmont Park in Philadelphia one day when he was thirteen years old. He stopped to watch two men painting a signboard. He was fascinated and, as he watched, a growing desire to be a painter grew within him. He watched the men paint for almost two hours and, when he went home, he reached a decision. He would become an artist.

His parents gave in to his desires and he attended the Philadelphia Academy of Fine Arts. He graduated in 1880.

During the next ten years, Henry worked at perfecting his skill. In 1889, he also learned photography which was a relatively new field of study. During this time, to add to his income, Henry became an instructor of Art at Clark University in Atlanta, Georgia.

At this time, the great desire of every artist was to study in Europe. Henry wanted to go to Rome to study, but he lacked the necessary money. In 1890, he held a large exhibit in Cleveland, Ohio. The art critics said that his paintings showed great promise. However, Henry became very discouraged as the days went by because he did not sell a single painting. Then, on the last day of the exhibit, Bishop and Mrs. Joseph C. Hartzell came to visit. They recognized his talent and bought his entire collection of pictures. Henry made enough money from this sale to leave for Europe.

In 1890, Henry left to make the grand tour of Europe. He stopped in Liverpool, London, and Paris. When Henry got to Paris, he fell in love with the city. He abandoned all thoughts of going to Rome. He stayed in Paris and began working.

Henry became interested in painting religious pictures. Perhaps he was interested in religious art because of his father's work. In 1869, he exhibited his painting of "Daniel in the Lion's Den." This painting won him many honors.

One year later, his "Resurrection of Lazarus" was displayed and was promptly purchased by the French government. This recognition was a great honor.

Henry was honored everywhere and received many awards and prizes. He was awarded a Medal of Honor at the Paris Exposition in 1900. He also returned to the United States to receive the Louisiana Purchase Prize in 1904. He then stayed in Philadelphia to visit with his parents and remained until 1906 when he received the Harris Prize from the Art Institute in Chicago. This prize was worth $500—a great sum of money at this time.

However, he was not happy at home. He missed Paris. He returned to Paris where he spent the rest of his life. He continued painting and turned out many masterpieces. Even though you may not have known Henry as the artist, you may have seen some of the masterpieces created by this artist. "Christ Walking on the Water", "The Disciples on the Road to Bethany", and "The Flight into Egypt" are a few of his great masterpieces. Henry lived the rest of his life in Paris and died there in 1937.

REMEMBERING HENRY OSSAWA TANNER

A. KNOWING YOUR VOCABULARY

sermons, 57 exhibit, 58

B. THINGS TO REMEMBER

1. Who decided to become a painter at the age of twelve?
2. How did Henry's father earn a living?
3. Where did Henry live in Europe?
4. What are the names of some of Henry's paintings?
5. What were the awards and honors Henry received?

C. THINGS TO THINK AND TALK ABOUT

1. Henry Tanner became a great painter. He decided to be a painter when he was very young. Have you ever wanted to paint? What? Have you ever wanted to dance? Why? Have you ever wanted to write? What? What would you like to do that you think you could do well?
2. Henry's parents did not understand his desire to paint. Have you ever wanted to do something that others did not understand? Did you still do it? What was it? Were you ever successful in helping anyone to understand? When?
3. Henry held an exhibit of his paintings. Have you ever done anything that was on exhibit for others to see? What was it?
4. Henry attended a special school to study art. Have you ever wanted to learn something that is not taught in your school? What kind of special school would you need to attend?
5. Henry enjoyed painting religious pictures. What kind of picture do you prefer to make?

D. THINGS TO DO

1. Draw a picture of Henry Tanner at his easel. Write a sentence under the picture describing what you think Henry is thinking while he is painting the picture.
2. Henry Tanner received many honors. Have you ever received any honors? Write a story about your honors or an honor received by someone in your family.
3. Henry felt that he must study art in Paris, France. What do you know about the city of Paris? What makes it a favorite place for artists to study? If you traveled to Paris, what would you like to see there?

E. BIBLIOGRAPHY

Butcher, Margaret Just. *The Negro In American Culture.* Alfred A. Knopf. 1956.

Hughes, Langston. *Famous American Negroes.* Dodd, Mead. 1954.

GEORGE WASHINGTON CARVER
(1864-1943)
Agricultural Chemist

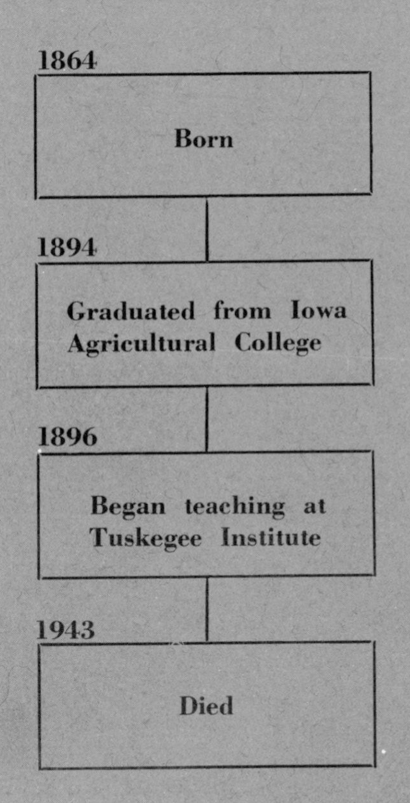

From my prison cell, I have watched America slowly coming awake. It is not fully awake yet, but there is soul in the air and everywhere I see beauty.

Eldridge Cleaver

MEETING GEORGE W. CARVER

George was born in a slave cabin on the Carver plantation. When he was almost a year old, a band of night riders stole George and his mother. The night riders were men who kidnapped slaves and sold them to other masters far away. They left little George under a tree because he was sick and crying. A man found little George and brought him back to Moses Carver.

George loved plants. Mr. Carver taught George many things about plants. He learned how to take care of them and make them grow. He was called a plant doctor.

George wanted to learn more about plants. He wanted to find a school. He said good-bye to the Carvers and left to find a school.

George lived with a lady named Mrs. Watkins while he went to school. He helped Mrs. Watkins on her farm. Mrs. Watkins taught George how to wash and iron clothes.

George learned all he could. Then he went away to college. He remembered what Mrs. Watkins had taught him and opened a laundry to help pay for his education.

He could also paint beautiful pictures. He sold many of his paintings.

George became a teacher. He taught his students how to make their crops grow better. He was a great man. He helped us all.

KNOWING GEORGE W.CARVER

George Washington Carver was born in Diamond Grove, Missouri. Soon after George was born, his father was run over by a wagon and killed. When he was almost a year old, a band of night riders stole George and his mother. The night riders were men who kidnapped slaves and sold them to other masters far away. George's brother escaped. George and his mother were taken into the mountains. Little George was sick. The night riders left him under a tree. They rode on with George's mother who was never seen again.

George was found and returned to his master, Moses Carver. The Carvers took George and his brother into their family.

While living with the Carvers, George became interested in plants. He learned how to take care of them and became known as a plant doctor. He wanted to go to school to learn more about plants. When he was 13 years old, he started out on his own to acquire more education.

George lived with a kind lady named Mrs. Watkins. He went to school and did housework for Mrs. Watkins. She also taught him how to wash and iron clothes.

When George went to college he remembered what Mrs. Watkins had taught him and opened a laundry to help pay for his education. When he finished work, he often painted pictures. He sold some of his paintings.

George graduated from Iowa Agricultural College in 1894. He was the first Afro-American to graduate from Iowa Agricultural College. George became a teacher at Iowa.

One day, Booker T. Washington came to speak at the

college. He asked George to come to Tuskegee Institute. In his laboratory George did many experiments. He did many experiments with the peanut and sweet potato. He discovered that many useful products could be made from each of these things.

George worked and experimented at Tuskegee until his death in 1943. He helped many, many people.

UNDERSTANDING GEORGE WASHINGTON CARVER

George Washington Carver was born in Diamond Grove, Missouri, in 1864. Shortly after George's birth his father was run over by a wagon and killed. When he was almost a year old, he and his mother were stolen by outlaws. The outlaws were a band of night riders who kidnaped slaves and sold them to other masters far away. George's older brother escaped, but George and his mother were taken by the night riders over the mountains into Arkansas. However, George was sick with whooping cough. They abandoned him under a tree.

George's master sent a man to search for the stolen slaves. The man found George under the tree. He brought the little boy back to Moses Carver. He was given a horse as a reward for finding the baby.

George was a very sick baby, but he was helped by the Carvers. The Carvers took George and his brother into their family. They loved the two boys, fed them, clothed them, and gave them an education. George grew up to be a very weak child. He was not strong enough to work in the fields so he learned to do housework. George became interested in plants while living with the Carvers. He learned how to take care of them and what made them grow. He became known as a plant doctor.

He wanted to go to school to learn more about plants. When George was about ten years old, his brother left home to work in a city. George was very lonesome. When he was 13, he started out on his own to find a school. He had only a pocket full of shiny stones and the clothes given to him by the Carvers. George lived with Mrs. Watkins in Neosha, which had a school for children. He had no trouble finding work because he knew how to clean a house and do household chores. Mrs. Watkins also taught George how to wash and iron. She also gave George a Bible. This book became George's proudest possession. Then he caught a ride into Kansas with a family that was moving there. He stayed in Kansas City and started high school there. His first job was in a laundry. He often painted pictures when he was finished with his work.

He found a home with the Seymour family and moved to Minneapolis with them. He had a chance to finish high school there. He worked at many jobs in order to finish his education.

George wanted to go to college, but there were not many colleges that took Afro-American students. George was finally accepted at Simpson College in September of 1890. George was now 25 years old. When he had paid his entrance fees, he had only ten cents left. He bought a nickel's worth of corn meal and a nickel's worth of beef suet.

George talked a storekeeper into letting him have two tin tubs, a washboard, soap, and some blueing on credit. Then he announced to his classmates that he was opening a laundry. George earned enough money from washing and ironing to pay for his first year of college.

George wanted to study art, but his teacher told him he should take studies that would help him get a job in later life. With his art teacher's help, George went to Iowa Agricultural College to study agriculture. However, he still did laundry work. Moreover, he received free meals in the kitchen in the cafeteria by serving students their meals. He also sold some of his paintings. One painting won honorable mention at the Chicago World's Fair of 1894. His graduating class made him poet laureate—the best poet in the class—and called him doctor because he was such a brilliant student. He was the first Afro-American to graduate from Iowa Agricultural College.

After graduation, George taught for two years on the

faculty at the college and worked on his master's degree. He received this degree in 1896. During these two years George had received many offers to teach at southern colleges. Booker T. Washington came to speak at the college. He met George and was very impressed with his work. He offered him a job at Tuskegee Institute, as head of the Department of Agriculture, director of agricultural research, and teacher of natural sciences. It was a heavy program but George accepted the job at Tuskegee and remained there for the rest of his life.

George started his class with only 13 students but had 76 students by the end of the first year. George taught his students and the farmers around Tuskegee how to grow better crops. He made a fertilizer that made the clay soil turn into a rich and fertile soil. George also completed many experiments in his laboratory. He found that by planting crops other than cotton, the soil would not wear out as fast. He did many experiments with the peanut and the sweet potato. He found that many useful products could be made from these things. He made flour, vinegar, shoe polish, a type of rubber, molasses, starch, imitation ginger, library paste, wood filler, rope, instant coffee, and almost a hundred other products from sweet potatoes. He made paint from Alabama clay and used sawdust to make marbles. He made insulation wallboard from cornstalks. He made plastics from wood-shavings and writing paper from the wisteria vines which grew along the countryside. He developed linoleum, metal polish, vegetable-milk, ink, grease, cooking oils, 19 shades of dyes and stains, food sauces, shampoo, peanut butter and cheese from peanut extractions. He also published 100 cooking recipes using the peanut as a base. Using these recipes, a full-course dinner could be served.

George's experiments with the peanut gave the South a two million dollar business. As a result, Congress passed a tariff law to protect American peanuts. George was called to Washington to testify before Congress would pass the tariff law. He was given ten minutes to tell what he had done with the peanut. Once he began talking and explaining, the congressmen let him talk for over two hours because they were interested and amazed.

Many universities awarded George Washington Carver honorary degrees—the University of Rochester in Rochester, New York, awarded him a Doctor of Science degree.

George met many famous people. President Franklin D. Roosevelt visited him at Tuskegee. They became good friends. Thomas A. Edison was also a good friend. Moreover, Henry Ford offered George $50,000 a year to work in his laboratories.

George became famous rather than rich because he refused to take money for his work. George died in 1943.

REMEMBERING GEORGE WASHINGTON CARVER

A. KNOWING YOUR VOCABULARY

night riders, 66 laboratory, 67
experimented, 67 agricultural, 70

B. THINGS TO REMEMBER

1. Where was George Washington Carver born?
2. What happened when George was one year old?
3. Why did George leave the Carvers at the age of thirteen?
4. What are some of the products Prefessor Carver developed from the sweet potato?

C. THINGS TO THINK AND TALK ABOUT

1. When George was a baby, he was separated from his mother. Have you ever been separated from your family or friends? How did you feel? Have you ever been lost? How did you feel while you were lost? How did you feel when you were found?
2. George was called the "plant doctor". What would you like to be called? Why? What would you not like to be called? Why?
3. George left the Carvers in order to obtain an education. Why did he have to leave home for an education? Would you ever leave home for some reason? What? How can you get an education? Will you ever have to leave home to complete your education?
4. George was a great scientist. He discovered many things. Have you ever dreamed of discovering anything? What is it?
5. Mrs. Watkins gave George a Bible. He kept this

book for 70 years. Why do you think George treasured this book? Have you ever owned anything of value? Why was it of value to you? Does something have to cost a lot of money in order to be treasured by a person? Why? Why not?

D. THINGS TO DO

1. List the many things Dr. Carver made from the peanut and the sweet potato. Prepare a display of the products listed.
2. Assemble a nature book. Collect pressed wild and domestic flowers, roots, stems, leaves and seeds.Then label each specimen that you have collected.
3. List adjectives or phrases that could be used in describing a man of George Washington Carver's stature.

e.g. loving	humble	lover of nature
kind	appreciative	lover of God
grateful	brilliant	thoughtful
hard worker	important	ambitious

E. BIBLIOGRAPHY

Bontemps, Arna. *The Story of George Washington Carver*. Grosset and Dunlap. 1954.

Elliott, Lawrence. *George Washington Carver: The Man Overcame*. Prentice Hall. 1966.

Epstein, Samueland Beryl. *George Washington Carver: Negro Scientist*. Garrard Press. 1960.

Leipold, L.E., Ph.D. *Famous American Negroes - Famous American Heroes and Leader Series*. Denison. 1968.

Means, Florence. *Carver's George*. Houghton Mifflin. 1952.

MATTHEW A. HENSON
(1866-1955)
Explorer

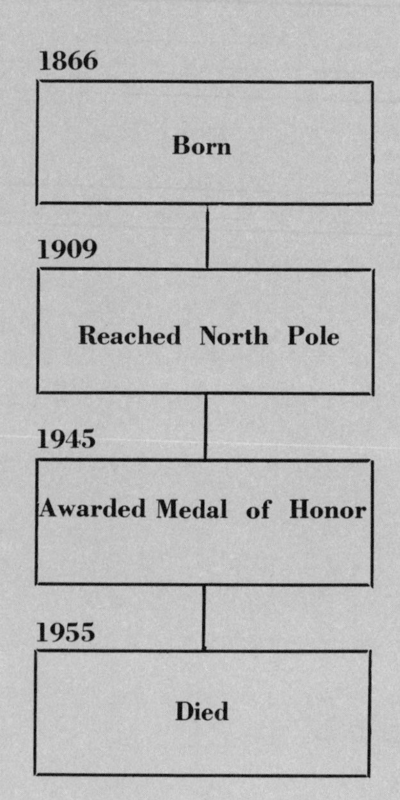

He (Henson) was the most popular man aboard the ship with the Eskimos. He could talk their language like a native. He made all the sleds which went to the Pole. He made all the stoves. Henson, the colored man went to the Pole with Peary because he was a better man than any of his white assistants. . .

Donald MacMillan
Member of Peary's Expedition

MEETING MATTHEW A. HENSON

It was dark. Matthew tiptoed out of the house. He walked down the road. Matthew Henson said, "I am thirteen years old. I want to see the world."

Matthew walked and walked. He came to a place where he saw many big ships. "I would like a job," he said to the captain of one of the ships. The captain gave Matthew a job helping the cook. The captain took Matthew to see many faraway countries.

One day he met a sailor named Lt. Peary. "I want to be the first man to get to the North Pole," he said to Matthew.

"I can help you," said Matthew. "I have learned all about sailing."

The two men had to travel very far. It was dark and cold and windy. It snowed and snowed. After many hard days and nights, the two men reached the North Pole.

"I will put up the American Flag," said Matthew. "Then everyone will know we got here first."

When they got home, Matthew wrote a book about his adventures.

KNOWING MATTHEW A. HENSON

Matthew was excited all day. He couldn't wait for night to come. When it was dark, he tiptoed out of the house and started to walk down the road. Matthew Henson had set out to see the world.

A friendly woman in Washington, D.C., let Matthew work as a dishwasher. He worked at night and went to school during the day. As he studied and worked he dreamed about sailing on a great ship to see the world. He read about the big boats in Baltimore, Maryland. Matthew walked to Baltimore to see the ships.

When he reached the docks in Baltimore he saw the sails of a large ship. It was called the "Katie Hines". The ship's captain gave Matthew a job. He helped the cook serve the captain's food. Captain Childs liked Matthew. He knew Matthew wanted to learn about sailing. Captain Childs became Matthew's teacher. He taught Matthew about sailing and took him to see many faraway countries. Matthew sailed with Captain Childs on the "Katie Hines" for five years.

Matthew then left the sea and returned to Washington, D.C. One day he met a sailor named Lt. Peary. Matthew Henson and Lt. Peary made many trips and explored many places together.

Lt. Peary wanted to be the first man to reach the North Pole. He asked Matthew to help him. The trip was very dangerous. The men had to live through very cold winds and heavy snow storms. They met Eskimos who showed them how to drive dog sleds, build igloos, hunt seal and bear, and how to make clothes from animal skins.

On April 6, 1909, the wish of the two men came

true. They arrived at the North Pole. Matthew raised the American Flag at the North Pole.

Matthew Henson wrote a book about his adventures. Moreover, he received a silver medal for his bravery.

UNDERSTANDING MATTHEW HENSON

At thirteen, Matthew wanted to see faraway places. He daydreamed about sailing on a great ship, so he decided to go for another long walk. This time he walked from Washington, D.C. to Baltimore, Maryland.

When Matthew reached the docks, he saw the masts of the "Katie Hines". After a while, he asked the captain for a job and got it.

Matthew's job was to help the cook and serve the Captain's food. Matthew, being a curious boy, started looking through the Captain's books. Captain Childs let him read the books and taught him history, mathematics, and navigation. Matthew sailed on the ship for five years. It traveled to China, Russia, Japan, Africa, and many other countries. Matthew made friends with the people who lived in these countries and learned their languages. He also learned to follow their customs.

After Captain Childs died, Matthew worked on a fishing boat for a short time.

He decided to return to Washington, D.C., to look for work. He found a job there as a stockroom clerk in a men's clothing store. While working there, Lt. Robert Peary came to the store to buy supplies for a trip to Nicaragua. He was looking for a man to travel with him to be his valet. He asked Matthew to go along. Matthew still had the desire to travel, so he agreed to go.

Lt. Peary's job was to survey the land for a new canal. Matthew helped by taking care of Peary's clothes and preparing food for the other men. Peary often asked Matthew to help with the surveying. Matthew enjoyed doing this kind of work.

When they returned to the United States, Peary asked

Matthew to go with him on his next trip to Greenland.

The trip on board the "Kite" was not an easy one. The men had to fight sickness, storms, and the ice floes in the water. Peary broke his leg during one of the storms.

When they arrived Peary asked some Eskimos to go with him on the expedition.

The Eskimos showed Matthew how to drive dog sleds, build igloos, hunt seal, bear and musk oxen, and make clothes from animal skins. Matthew learned how to speak the Eskimo language so he could trade knives and kitchen utensils for the Eskimos' dogs. As a result, the Eskimos treated Matthew as a brother and invited him to their igloos. They nicknamed him "Miy Palok" which means—"Dear Little Matthew."

Peary wanted to be the first man to get to the North Pole. Peary and Matthew Henson made eight trips before they reached the Pole.

Each trip was more difficult than the previous one. The men had to live through below zero temperatures, cold winds, blizzards, frost-bite, and hunger. At times the ice cracked under their feet and they had to pull themselves out. A few of the men died. Even Matthew and Peary suffered frostbite.

After each trip, Peary would make a lecture tour trying to raise money for the next trip. Matthew worked in the Arctic section of the Museum of Natural History in New York City.

The last trip they made was the most dangerous. Matthew fell through a crack in the ice and had to be rescued, but Matthew, Peary and four Eskimos continued on their way. On April 6, 1909, they reached the North Pole. Matthew raised the American Flag on the spot and they took photographs of the historic event.

When they returned to the United States, Peary received many awards and spoke to many groups of people about their experiences. Peary really knew that without Matthew he could not have survived and reached the North Pole. Both

Peary and Matthew wrote books about their adventures. Matthew called his book *Negro Explorer at the North Pole*. While writing the book, he worked parking automobiles. Later, he was a messenger in the New York Customs House until retirement.

Matthew was allowed to become a member of the Explorers Club in 1937. Finally, in 1945, Congress awarded him a silver medal for bravery. He died in 1955.

REMEMBERING MATTHEW HENSON

A. KNOWING YOUR VOCABULARY

North Pole, 75 floes, 79
temperatures, 79 blizzards, 79

B. THINGS TO REMEMBER

1. Who ran away from home to see the world when he was only eleven years old?
2. What city did Matthew visit?
3. Why did Matthew go to Baltimore?
4. Who was the explorer Matthew met?
5. How did Matthew contribute to our nation's history?

C. THINGS TO THINK AND TALK ABOUT

1. Matthew left home when he was eleven years old. If you were leaving home to see the world, what places would you visit? Where would you go first?
2. Matthew met Lieutenant Peary and joined his expedition to the North Pole. What would you like to explore? What subjects in school would help you if you wanted to be an explorer?
3. Matthew was the first man to reach the North Pole. How do you think he felt? Have you ever been the first person to do anything? What was it? How

did you feel?

4. When Matthew left home to see the world, he worked during the night and went to school during the day. Have you ever had to work very hard for something you wanted very badly? Tell us about it!
5. Matthew traveled to many far-away countries. What far-away places have you ever seen in books or on television?

D. THINGS TO DO

1. Select one of the following topics for reaction.
   How Does It Feel To Be Cold?
   How Does It Feel To Be Alone In The Dark?
   How Does It Feel To Discover Something?
   Younger children can talk about their feelings. Older children can write about their feelings.
2. Think and talk about words that describe Matthew Henson's experiences.

e.g. cold	shivery	discouraging
dark	unhappy	disillusioning
icy	frustrating	rewarding

E. BIBLIOGRAPHY

Leipold, L.E. Ph.D. *Famous American Negroes - Famous American Heroes and Leader Series.* Denison. 1968.

Ripley, Sheldon, *Matthew Henson Arctic Hero.* Houghton Mifflin. (Piper Book). 1968.

JAMES WELDON JOHNSON
(1871 - 1938)
Educator, Editor, Poet
Diplomat, Song Writer

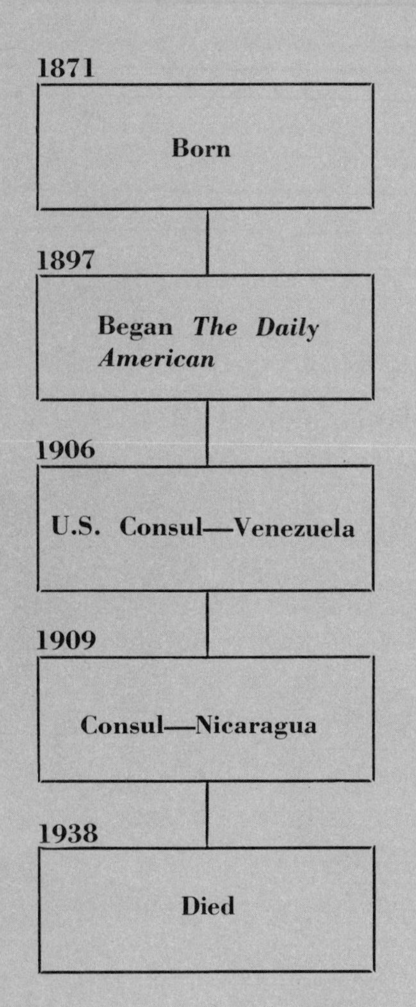

There's never been equality for me, nor freedom in this "homeland of the free."

Langston Hughes
Let America Be Free Again

MEETING JAMES WELDON JOHNSON

James Weldon Johnson was born in Jacksonville, Florida. When James was a little boy, he liked to write beautiful stories and poems. His mother gave him a big notebook so he could keep the stories and poems he wrote.

James loved music, too. His mother gave him piano lessons when he was just a little boy. James and his brother wrote a song for children to sing in school. The song is titled "Lift Every Voice and Sing." The song is so famous that many Afro-American children in the South still sing this song today.

James wrote many more songs. Some of the songs he wrote were sung in plays on the stage. He even wrote songs for the President of the United States.

James loved school. He learned many things and held many good jobs. He was the principal of a school. He worked for the government, and he was the first Afro-American lawyer in the state of Florida.

KNOWING JAMES WELDON JOHNSON

James was born on June 17, 1871, in Jacksonville, Florida. His father was the head waiter of a hotel. His mother was the first Negro woman to teach in the public schools of Florida. She taught James to play the piano when he was a little boy.

He liked to read and play baseball very much. He liked to write stories. He filled notebooks with the beautiful stories and poems.

He thought he wanted to be a doctor when he was a student in college. Instead, he became a teacher at Stanton elementary school. Soon he became principal. He added grades until his school included a four year high school.

James studied law for over a year and passed a very difficult examination. He became the first Afro-American lawyer in Florida.

For Lincoln's Birthday celebration, James and his brother wrote the words and music for a children's chorus. The song was titled "Lift Every Voice and Sing." The children sang the song when they left for college. It is still sung today in Afro-American schools and churches throughout the South.

James wrote songs for his brother's theater act. He wrote songs for Broadway shows in New York City. He wrote songs for the presidential campaign of Theodore Roosevelt. His poem "Creation" has been set to music and played by the Boston Symphony Orchestra.

In 1907, he was made consul for the United States at Puerto Cabello, Venezuela.

Later he was assigned to the United States Consul at Corinto, Nicaragua.

James Weldon Johnson became a professor of creative literature at Fisk University (a Negro college in Nashville, Tennessee) and a visiting professor of literature at New York University.

He was killed in an automobile accident in June, 1938.

UNDERSTANDING JAMES WELDON JOHNSON

James Weldon Johnson was born on June 17, 1871, in Jacksonville, Florida, to James Johnson and Helen Louise Dillette. During his lifetime, James was to become a teacher, a high school principal, a poet, a lawyer, a song writer, a diplomat, an editor, a librettist, a professor, and an administrator.

When James was born, his family had just moved into a new and very happy home. Sorrow came during the first year of his young life. His sister, Marie, older by a year and one half, died. When James was about three, things began to brighten. The St. James Hotel opened and Mr. Johnson became the head waiter at the hotel. James often went to work with his father. His father held the job for 13 years.

Also living with the family was Ricardo Rodriguez Ponce. Ricardo was a Spanish speaking Cuban boy who had come to the United States to learn English so he could enter college. When Ricardo entered Atlanta University, he could speak English very well and James spoke very good Spanish.

He spent his summers in various sections of Georgia teaching rural Black children their ABC's. James graduated from Atlanta University in 1894.

James returned to Jacksonville and became principal of the Stanton School. Stanton was an elementary school. When students reached the eighth grade, James Weldon Johnson encouraged them to continue working, and he set up special classes for them. He eventually made Stanton into a high school because he felt there was a need for more Negro high schools in the South. Stanton was the fourth Negro high school in the entire South.

While he was in Jacksonville, James also started a newspaper called "The Daily American." It was the first daily Afro-American newspaper in the United States.

James continued with his studies. He studied law and became the first Black American admitted to the Florida Bar.

James Weldon Johnson spent his limited spare time in writing poetry and free verse. His brother, J. Rosamund, returned from college and was very enthusiastic about the poetry. J. Rosamund had completed his music education and the two brothers decided to collaborate on some songs. Together they wrote the music and words for "Lift Every Voice and Sing". They used their first song on Lincoln's Birthday in 1900 at James' school.

The two brothers spent their summers in New York City writing music. When Stanton School burned down, James and his brother returned to New York City while waiting for the school to be rebuilt. They continued their song writing. From 1901-1906, they became two of the top composers of American popular music. James took time in 1904 to receive his Master's Degree from Atlanta University. While he was working in New York City, he took three years of graduate work at Columbia University.

James was very active politically and in 1906 was given the post of United States Consul at Puerto Cabello, Venezuela. James was transferred to Corinto, Nicaragua, in 1909. He married Grace Nail in 1911. James stayed in the consular service until 1914.

When James left the consular service, he became the editor of "The New York Age." The newspaper was one of the oldest Negro newspapers in New York. A Literary Doctorate Degree was conferred on him in 1917 by Talledega College and Howard University.

James became the field secretary of the NAACP in 1916. He was a busy administrator in this post.

Fisk University made James a Professor of Creative

Literature in 1930. New York University made him visiting professor in Creative Literature in 1934.

James Weldon Johnson died June 25, 1938, after a railroad train hit his car at a grade crossing near his summer home at Dark Harbor, Maine.

REMEMBERING JAMES WELDON JOHNSON

A. KNOWING YOUR VOCABULARY

Symphony Orchestra, 84 consul, 84
epidemic, 86 fluency, 86

B. THINGS TO REMEMBER

1. Where was James Weldon Johnson born?
2. What did James like to do as a small boy?
3. How did James serve the government?
4. What did James do after he left his government position?
5. How did James die?

C. THINGS TO THINK AND TALK ABOUT

1. James enjoyed many interests while he was a youngster. He liked to play the piano, read and play baseball. What are your hobbies and interests? What do you like best to do on Saturdays?
2. When James was young, he wanted to become a doctor. He became a teacher instead. Have you ever wanted to be something and then changed your mind as you grew older? What did you want to be when you were younger? What do you want to be now?
3. James wrote many songs. Many of his works received praise and fame. What have you ever done

that your mother praised? your father? your teacher? Have you ever written songs, stories, or poems? Do you like to write? Why?

4. James became the first Negro lawyer in the state of Florida. Have you ever been first at something? In what way would you like to be first?

D. THINGS TO DO

1. James spent his summers teaching young children their ABC's. Make a picture book of drawings of the things you do during your summers.
2. James Weldon Johnson worked in many different job areas. Discuss requirements in education and training for each of his jobs. Assemble pictures into a book—'Things We Could Be' or 'My Book of Jobs'.

E. BIBLIOGRAPHY

Ferguson, Blanche. *Countee Cullen And The Negro Renaissance*. Dodd, Mead. 1968.

Mettzer, Milton. *In their Own Words: A History Of The American Negro—1865-1916*. Thomas Y. Crowell Co. 1965.

PAUL LAURENCE DUNBAR
(1872-1906)
Lyric Poet

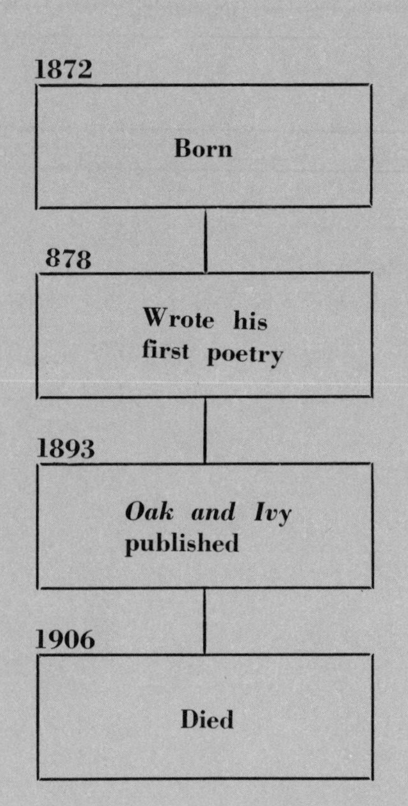

I doubt not God is good, well-meaning, kind. . . What awful brain compels His awful hand. Yet do I marvel at this curious thing: To make a poet black, and bid him sing!

Countee Cullen
Yet Do I Marvel

MEETING PAUL LAURANCE DUNBAR

"I wish I could, I wish I could, I wish I could read," said Mrs. Dunbar.

"I know I can, I know I can, I know I can read."

Some children in the neighborhood helped her. She did learn to read. It was hard work.

Paul's mother taught him how to read when he was only four years old. Paul liked to read. He would read and read. It made him feel happy.

One day Paul wrote some words. It was a poem. Paul was only six years old.

Every time he wrote a poem his mother would save it. She kept them in a shoe box.

Paul did very well in school. He wrote a song for his school.

Paul wanted to help his mother. He looked for a job. One day he found one. His first job was running an elevator.

He would work and read. Then he would write more poems. One day he sold some of his poems.

Friends told other people about the poet elevator boy. They came to see him.

Paul took his shoe box full of poems to a printing shop. The printer made the poems into a book. Paul sold the books and earned money. Soon many people knew him. Paul's home was in Dayton, Ohio.

KNOWING PAUL LAURENCE DUNBAR

Paul Laurence Dunbar was born in Dayton, Ohio. His mother, Matilda, could neither read nor write, but she was determined to learn. She would ask school children to teach her the alphabet. She learned quickly and soon could read sentences.

Joshua Dunbar was a plasterer. He also wanted to learn, so he taught himself.

Paul Laurence Dunbar was born on June 27, 1872. His father called him Paul because he had read in the Bible that Paul has a noble character.

When Paul was four, his mother taught him to read. He wrote his first poems when he was only six years old. His mother was very proud of him and encouraged him to continue writing.

Paul began sending poems to the newspapers. After people began reading his poems, he decided to write a book. *Oak and Ivy* was Paul Laurence Dunbar's first book. His poems were read and loved by people for many years.

UNDERSTANDING PAUL LAURENCE DUNBAR

Paul Laurence Dunbar was born in Dayton, Ohio, on June 27, 1872. His parents, Joshua Dunbar and Matilda Murphy, came from Kentucky where they had once been slaves.

His mother, Matilda, worked in a master's home and was kindly treated. The master read to his wife every evening and Matilda was allowed to sit on the floor at his knees and listen. She was so interested in the stories and poems that she did not want to go to bed. Poetry seemed to sing songs to her.

When the slaves were given their freedom, Matilda moved to Dayton, Ohio. In Dayton, she met Joshua Dunbar. He had been a slave. His master had been so cruel that Joshua had run away to Canada. When he heard of the Emancipation Proclamation, he came to Dayton. Not long after they met, Matilda and Joshua were married.

Matilda could neither read nor write, but she was determined to learn. She would coax the children to teach her the alphabet. She learned quickly and soon could read sentences. She could now read the Bible and the poetry she loved.

Joshua Dunbar was a plasterer. He was an old man when he married, and he could neither read nor write. He wanted to learn so he taught himself. He especially liked history and the biographies of great men. Mr. and Mrs. Dunbar educated themselves after they were married.

Paul Laurence Dunbar was born on June 27, 1872. His father called him Paul because he read in the Bible that Paul had a noble character.

Paul was their only child. When he was only four, his mother taught him to read. He was far ahead of the other children in his class when he started school. He liked school and enjoyed reading and spelling. The teacher would often find Paul reading while the other children were playing.

Paul was educated in the public schools. He was the only black student in his class at Steel High School. He was very popular with his classmates and became president of the literary society and editor of the student newspaper. He also wrote his Senior Class graduation song.

Paul's hopes of becoming a lawyer vanished when his father died while Paul was still in high school. He had to help support his mother. She tried to make a living by doing laundry work. Every evening Paul delivered the wash. After graduation he became an elevator operator at $4.00 per week.

During this period, a poem of his would occasionally appear in the local papers.

Paul's first book of poems, *Oak and Ivy*, was published in 1893, at his own expense. This small edition was printed at a cost of about $125. The book did not make him rich, but it gained for him much recognition in the literary world. He brought out more books as rapidly as he could write them. He became a popular lecturer and gave poetry readings. His lectures took him abroad. Upon returning home, he took a position in the Library of Congress where he worked until 1898.

On March 6, 1898, he married Alice Moore. She was an author and teacher in New York City.

Paul Laurence Dunbar died when he was only 34 years old. He was victim of tuberculosis. His home in Dayton is maintained today as a public landmark.

Paul Laurence Dunbar was a lyric writer. He had a special gift for capturing the musical quality of Afro-American speech. He deserves a place in American literature as one man who did much to further the achievements of later twentieth century writers.

REMEMBERING PAUL LAURENCE DUNBAR

A. KNOWING YOUR VOCABULARY
   elevator, 91   alphabet, 92
   published, 95

B. THINGS TO REMEMBER
   1. How did Paul's parents learn to read?
   2. How old was Paul when he first began writing poems? What was Paul's first job? The title of Paul's first book of poems?
   3. What did Paul do after he gained recognition from his first book?
   4. Where did Paul work for the government?
   5. How old was Paul when he died?

C. THINGS TO THINK AND TALK ABOUT
   1. Mr. Dunbar named his son Paul because he had read in the Bible that Paul was a noble man. Did your parents select your name for a special reason? Why are you proud of your name?
   2. Paul wrote poems when he was very young. His mother kept them in a shoe box. Does your mother or father keep the things you do in a special place? Where do you keeep your own treasures? What are some of the things you treasure most?
   3. Paul accepted a job running an elevator. He worked to help his mother. Have you ever worked to help someone other than yourself? What did you do?
   4. Paul's parents learned to read when they were no longer children. Do you know any adults who are

attending school? Why do you think adults attend school?

D. THINGS TO DO

1. Paul Laurence Dunbar worked in the Library of Congress. Discuss the job requirements and job duties of a librarian. Invite the school or local librarian to visit the class as a resource person. Save unanswered or unresolved questions for the visitor.
2. Discuss the services of a library. What skills are necessary in order to use the library successfully? Plan a field trip to the local library.

E. BIBLIOGRAPHY

Brawley, Benjamin. *Paul Laurence Dunbar, Poet of His People*. Chapel Hill. 1936.

Gould, Jean. *That Dunbar Boy*, Mead. 1968.

Muir, John. *Famous American Negro Writers*. Dodd, Mead. 1968.

Rollins, Charlomad. *Famous American Negro Poets*. Dodd, Mead. 1965.

MARY McLEOD BETHUNE
(1875-1955)
Educator

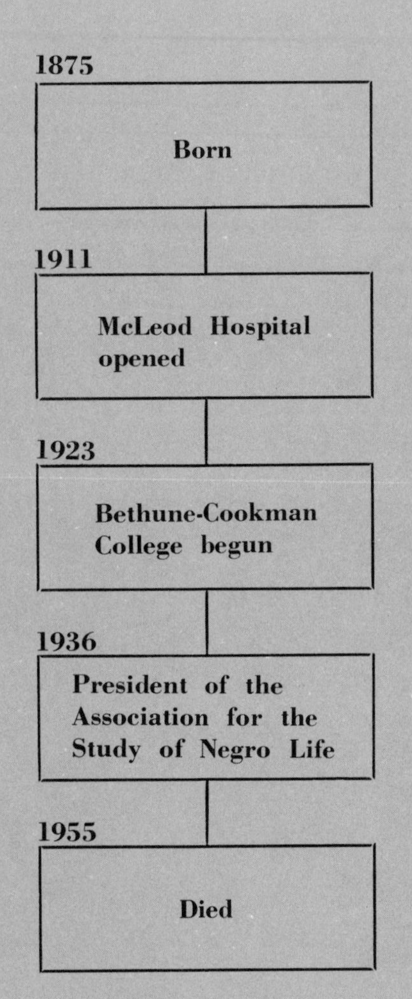

Religion, nationality, and language are a part of our social, not our biological heritage. . . . A person's race thus tells us nothing at all about his religion, his nationality, his language or his manners and morals.

Ina C. Brown
On Race

MEETING MARY McLEOD BETHUNE

One day, when she came in from picking cotton in the fields, Mary Bethune said to the other little girls who were working with her, "When I grow up, I'm going to be a teacher."

"Let's play school," said her little friends. They had fun. One little girl said to Mary, "You are a good teacher."

When she was older, she really did have a school of her own under a tree. She used boxes for desks and chairs. She did not have pencils, but she made some from burned pieces of logs. Many people wanted their children to attend her school because there were few good schools in the South.

Sometimes the dreams a little girl hopes for come true. Mary Bethune worked hard to save money. Many people helped her get enough money to buy land. She built a school on this land. The President of the United States, President Roosevelt, heard about the wonderful work she was doing. He invited her to the White House to talk about more schools for all the children in the South.

Mary Bethune's little school became a big college. Her little dream turned out to be a giant dream.

Many little girls that read about Mary Bethune would like to be like her. Everyone says, "She was the little girl teacher who grew up to be a famous teacher."

KNOWING MARY McLEOD BETHUNE

Mary McLeod Bethune was born in Mayesville, South Carolina in 1875. Mary worked very hard when she was a child. She picked cotton in the fields and helped her mother do washing for other families.

While Mary was delivering laundry one day, she found a picture book. She could not read the book. She wanted to read very much.

Mary soon got a chance to attend school. A church opened a school for Afro-Americans about five miles from Mary's home. Mary went to this school for six years.

When she graduated she wanted to get more education, but the family's mule died and Mary had to stay home and work. She had to pull the plow in place of the mule. It seemed as if Mary would never go to school again.

Then something wonderful happened! Mary received a scholarship to enter school again.

When Mary finished college, she became a teacher. She taught in Augusta, Georgia, and Sumter, South Carolina. It was in Sumter that she met and married Albertus Bethune. Shortly after their marriage Mr. Bethune died. Mary wanted to open a school for Afro-American girls. She found a place to open her school near the city dump. She opened her school on October 3, 1904. She had five girls and her son in her first class.

The girls learned to cook, sew, read, write and do arithmetic. Mary's school grew and grew. Mary's school joined the Cookman Institute for boys in 1923. That school became known as the Bethune-Cookman College.

Mary McLeod Bethune did many things for her people. She also opened a hospital for Afro-Americans. She received many honors and trophies for her work.

Mary spent her life helping people, especially young people.

UNDERSTANDING MARY McLEOD BETHUNE

Mary McLeod Bethune was born in Mayesville, South Carolina, July 10, 1875. Her home was a four room cabin that was shared by ten other members of her family.

Mary was a hard worker as a child. She worked in the fields picking cotton.

Mary soon received a chance to enter school. The Missionary Board of a church opened a school for blacks about five miles from Mary's home. Mary was glad to walk five long miles to learn to read and write. She walked this distance for six years until she graduated from the Missionary School.

Mary wanted to continue her education, but the family needed her. It seemed as if Mary would never go to school again, even though she was only twelve years old.

Then something wonderful happened! Mary got a chance to go to school once more. A lady seamstress offered a scholarship to one of the students at Mayesville to attend Scotia School in North Carolina. Mary received the scholarship and left home for school again.

In North Carolina, Mary thought about becoming a missionary in Africa. When she left Scotia, she was awarded another scholarship to Moody Institute in Chicago, Illinois.

Mary stayed in Chicago for two years. She was chief vocalist on the gospel team. She also did some preaching.

After her studies were complete, Mary decided to become a teacher. She first taught in Augusta, Georgia, and then in Sumter, South Carolina.

It was in Sumter that she met and married Albertus Bethune. They moved to Savannah, Georgia. Then they moved to Palatka, Florida, with their small son. Mary Bethune died there.

For many years Mary wanted to establish a school for girls where she could teach useful things. She found a great need for her services at Daytona, Florida.

Mary was greatly needed because many Afro-Americans were unable to get an education because of the lack of schools.

Mary found a place to open her school near the city dump.

On October 3, 1904, Mary's school was officially opened under a tree with five girls and her son sitting on orange crates. It was called the Daytona Educational Industrial Training School for Negro Girls. The parents were asked to pay 50 cents a week for tuition.

Girls learned to cook, sew, read, write and do arithmetic. A choir was organized to raise money to improve the building they had erected.

In two years, Mrs. Bethune had four teachers and 250 students in her school. Her school was growing. Mary's school merged in 1923 with the Cookman Institute for Boys and became known as the Bethune-Cookman College.

Mary was concerned about another problem of the Afro -American. No hospital would accept a Black when he was ill. Mary decided that the Black Americans must have a hospital. The McLeod Hospital opened with only two beds in 1911. The hospital grew to a well-equipped building with twenty beds and a staff of doctors and student nurses. The hospital remained open for twenty years.

As a leading educator, Mrs. Bethune spoke to many people. She was chosen to serve on the Advisory Committee of the National Youth Administration Program. She served for more than twenty years as a special advisor on minority affairs to Presidents Franklin D. Roosevelt and Harry S. Truman.

She received many honors, citations, and trophies for her work. Among her honors were the coveted Spingarn

Gold Medal, an honorary degree of Doctor of Humanities, and Presidency of the Association for the Study of Negro Life and History.

Mary spent her life helping children and young people. Many of these people grew up to help others.

REMEMBERING MARY McLEOD BETHUNE

A. KNOWING YOUR VOCABULARY

college, 99 trophies, 101

B. THINGS TO REMEMBER

1. Who helped Mary continue her schooling?
2. What did Mary decide to become when she finished college?
3. Where did Mary begin teaching?
4. Where did Mary open her school?
5. What were Mary's contributions to our nation's history?

C. THINGS TO THINK AND TALK ABOUT

1. Mary found a picture book when she was a little girl. What is your favorite picture or book?
2. Mary had to walk five miles to get to school each day. What hardships have you had to go through in order to obtain something you wanted very much?
3. Mary received a scholarship from a woman to help her get a further education. Who has helped you in school? How?

D. THINGS TO DO

1. Play school. Choose a teacher and children. Plan a dramatization of Mary McLeod Bethune's life as a little girl with her friends playing school. Write with charcoal. Use home-made books and

boxes for chairs.

2. Write a short story using one of these titles:
   A. Mary Bethune As A Little Girl
   B. Mary Bethune's First School
   C. Mary Bethune Was Called A Giant
   D. Why Mary Bethune Became Famous
3. Write a sentence about Mary Bethune using each of the following words:

hospitals	White House	Florida
money	dream	burned wood
help	schools	college

4. Design a hospital such as the one which Mary dreamed of for her people.

E. BIBLIOGRAPHY

Carruth, Ella Kaiser. *She Wanted To Read: The Story of Mary McLeod Bethune*. Abington Press. 1966.

Fleming, Alice. *Great Women Teachers*. J.B. Lippincott & Co. 1965.

PERCY LANON JULIAN
(1899 -   )
Research Chemist

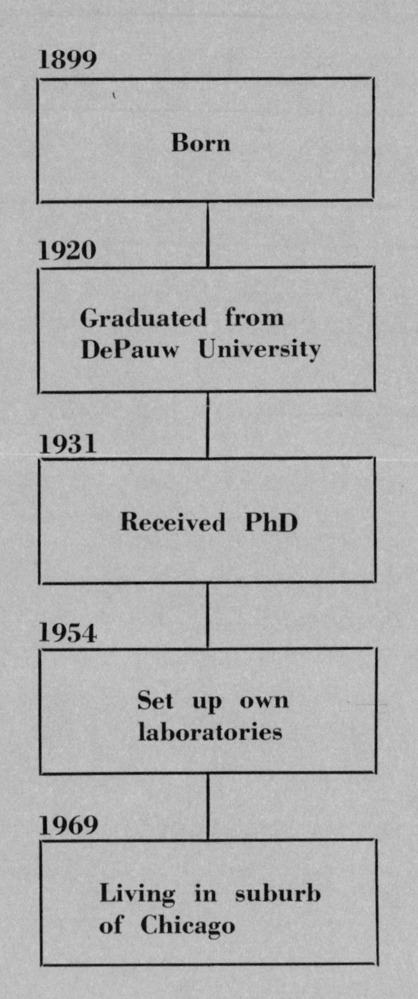

Had it not been for the Negro school and college, the Negro would, to all intents and purposes, have been driven back to slavery.

William E. Burghardt DuBois
Black Reconstruction

MEETING PERCY LANON JULIAN

"Percy," said Mother, "what are you going to be when you get big?"

Percy thought and thought about what he wanted to be when he grew up. "I wish I could be something wonderful," he said.

One day, Percy Julian was walking home from school.

Percy saw an open window. Inside were many boys and girls. Percy climbed a fence and listened. The boys and girls were working. They were doing things he had never seen anyone do before. He saw them make water turn red. Then the water turned blue. After that the water turned green.

He wanted to stay and watch for a long time, but had to go home.

Percy knew now what he wanted to be when he was big.

Percy said, "Oh Mother, do you think I could ever be a chemist?"

"Yes, Percy, I think you can, but you will have to work hard," said mother.

Percy went to school for many years. He learned many things. He became a chemist. He was a wonderful chemist. He did wonderful things. He helped make medicine for sick people. He helped make something to put out fires. He made many things that helped people.

Percy Lanon Julian did become something wonderful. His wish had come true.

KNOWING PERCY LANON JULIAN

Percy Lanon Julian was born in Montgomery, Alabama. Percy's hometown had a school for Afro-American children but it only had eight grades. When black children finished at this school, their education was usually complete. However, Percy wanted to attend high school. He enrolled in a small school that trained teachers and received his high school education there.

When Percy finished high school, he went to college to learn about chemistry. His whole family moved to Greencastle, Indiana, so Percy's brothers and sisters could benefit from a better education.

After Percy graduated from DePauw University in Greencastle, Indiana, he obtained a job teaching chemistry at Fisk University. He studied chemistry at a university in Vienna, Austria. When he returned to the United States, he began teaching chemistry at Harvard University in Boston, Massachusetts.

Percy then worked in a chemistry laboratory with a big manufacturing company. He discovered many things. He discovered medicines, a substance for making paint watertight, and a foam to put out fires.

Percy became a successful student, teacher, and chemist. Today, Percy Julian is still working to help to make everyone's life better.

UNDERSTANDING PERCY JULIAN

Percy Julian was destined to become a successful industrial chemist despite many serious obstacles which faced him. Even though many avenues in the chemical industry were closed to him, he opened those avenues through hard work and persistence to achieve the goal which he had set.

Percy was born on April 11, 1899, in Montgomery, Alabama. He was the oldest of six children.

Percy's father had been educated in a mission school, and his mother was a school teacher. Both worked very hard for their children. Percy learned from them the meaning of hard work and, above all, the value of an education.

The Julians' home town had a school for Negro children, but it only had eight grades. When children finished at this school, their education was usually completed. To compensate for the lack of a high school for Negro children, Percy attended a small teacher training school in order to receive the equivalent of a high school education.

In 1916, Percy was accepted at DePauw University in Greencastle, Indiana. He worked in chemical research.

Percy's formal schooling had been so poor that he was required to carry extra subjects during his first two years at the university. He record was so good during his four years that he was honored as valedictorian of his class.

Since few industrial jobs or graduate fellowships were forthcoming, Percy accepted a job at Fisk University as a chemistry teacher. His approach was so stimulating that the dean of the school complimented him.

While teaching at Fisk, Percy applied for a fellowship at Harvard. He was accepted and received his Master's Degree with a high scholastic record.

Upon graduating from Harvard, he taught at West Virginia State College for a year and then accepted an invitation from Harvard University to develop a lab there.

Percy decided to pursue additional study and enrolled in the University of Vienna where he obtained his Doctor's Degree in 1931.

Returning to the United States, Percy Julian started a scientific project at Harvard University but shortly thereafter went to DePauw to work in the chemistry research department.

Percy Julian then turned to industry and accepted a position with a company in Chicago. At the time he accepted a position with them, the company was doing work on the soybean and wanted Percy to help them. Percy's research led to the discovery of several synthetic substances which could be used in paint to make it water tight, and a drug named cortisone, which helped alleviate the pain caused by arthritis. Additional research brought about the discovery of a foam which was used to smother fires. These are only a few of the discoveries Percy Julian made.

In 1954, Percy Julian set up his own laboratories and, in 1961, merged with a pharmaceutical firm in Philadelphia.

He is currently living in a suburb of Chicago, and is continuing to do research to make everyone's life more comfortable.

REMEMBERING PERCY LANON JULIAN

A. KNOWING YOUR VOCABULARY
   chemistry, 107   manufacturing, 108
   pharmaceutical, 111

B. THINGS TO REMEMBER
   1. What did Percy think he might want to be when he grew up?
   2. Why did Percy decide to become a chemist?
   3. Where did Percy attend high school?
   4. Where did Percy attend college?
   5. What were Percy's contributions to our nation's history?

C. THINGS TO THINK AND TALK ABOUT
   1. When Percy was a small child, he could not decide what he wanted to be when he grew up. What are some of the things you are thinking of becoming? Why?
   2. Percy observed some chemistry students through a window. They were experimenting with chemicals of many different colors. Percy was excited by what he saw. Have you ever visited a place or seen anything that gave you an idea of what you wanted to do when you were older? What did you see? Where were you at the time?
   3. Percy became a famous inventor and chemist. He invented many things that improved living for people. Have you ever thought of inventing something to improve life for people? What would it be? What are some of the jobs that help to make life better for people?
   4. The dean at the University tried to discourage

Percy from following a chemistry career because there were few people in this field. Have you ever known anyone who has accomplished something even when others tried to discourage him? Is it difficult to know when you should listen to others and when you should listen to yourself?

5. The Julian family moved to DePauw so that Percy's brothers and sisters could receive a good education. What do people in your family do so that you can receive a good education—so that you will be happy?

D. THINGS TO DO

1. Plan a mural or art display using Percy Julian's life as a theme.
2. Write a paragraph on 'Why Education is Important'.

E. BIBLIOGRAPHY

Asimov, Isaac. *Break Throughs In Science*. Houghton, Mifflin Co. 1959.

LANGSTON HUGHES
(1902-1967)
Poet and Author

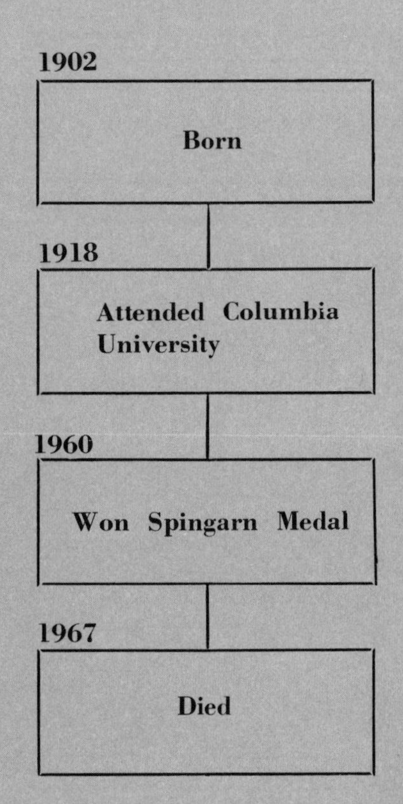

The night is beautiful
So the faces of my people.

The stars are beautiful
So the eyes of my people.

Beautiful, also is the sun
Beautiful, also are the souls of my people.

Langston Hughes
My People

MEETING LANGSTON HUGHES

Langston looked at the boys and girls playing in the school yard. He could not play. "Why don't they like me?" Langston asked his grandmother.

"Some people don't like blacks," his grandmother said.

Langston was very sad. He wrote a poem about the sad feeling he had. His teacher liked his poem and encouraged him to write more poems.

One day, Langston heard about a famous poet who was visiting the hotel where Langston worked. Langston showed his poems to the famous poet. The famous poet put Langston's picture and poem in the newspaper. Everyone began reading the poems by Langston Hughes.

He won many prizes for his good writing. He helped show the hard life of Afro-Americans.

KNOWING LANGSTON HUGHES

Langston Hughes was born on February 1, 1902, in Missouri. When he was a little boy, he lived with his mother in Kansas. When he was old enough to go to school, his mother sent him to a school where most of the children were white. Langston was an Afro-American. It was not easy to be the only different child in a group.

Almost everyone was good and kind to Langston, but sometimes there were people who were not kind. Once, when this happened, a white boy broke through the crowd and helped him. He said, "Run! Run as fast as you can while I stop the boys!"

Langston never forgot this boy. Not all white people are cruel to Blacks. There are white people who will fight for the Afro-American.

His teachers helped him with poetry. He learned to love poetry and write poems of his own. He wrote the best poems of his class in high school. The boys and girls chose him to be the class poet.

His father said that he could go to college. He went to Columbia University. However, he had to quit school.

He did not obtain a good job. All he could find was a job as a bus boy in Washington, picking up dirty dishes.

He met a famous writer who liked his poems so much that the writer told everyone how good Langston's poems were. His picture was in the newspaper, and people called him "The Negro Boy Poet." He was famous. He wrote and wrote. He wrote poems; he wrote stories; he wrote plays; he wrote articles for the newspapers. He won many prizes for his good writing.

Langston Hughes lived in New York City and is now

very famous for the things he wrote. He died in 1967.

UNDERSTANDING LANGSTON HUGHES

Langston Hughes was born February 1, 1902, in Joplin, Missouri, but grew up in Lawrence, Kansas.

When Langston was ready to start school he was living with his mother in Topeka, Kansas. They lived in a room in the downtown section of the city. His mother took him to the nearest school. This school was attended by white children and some of them did not want Langston Hughes at their school. Mrs. Hughes went to the school board and told them it was not fair of them to send her son several blocks away to a Negro school. The school-board then agreed to let Langston enter the school near his home. Most of his teachers were nice to him except one teacher who would sometimes insult him because he was an Afro-American.

There were times when several children would throw stones and tin cans at Langston. Not all of the children treated him this way. There was one boy who would always stick up for him and Langston never forgot this boy. He learned early that not all white people disliked Black Americans.

When Langston was in the second grade, his mother took him to his grandmother's house. There he lived until he was twelve years old. Langston was very unhappy and lonely. His grandmother was very poor.

One summer, a friend of Langston's mother sent her son to visit Langston for a few weeks, but the little boy only stayed a few days. Then he wrote to his mother that he wanted to leave because Langston's grandmother served nothing but salt pork and dandelions for food. Langston cried when the boy showed the letter to him because the boy was right. He never wanted anyone to visit him again.

Being alone most of the time, Langston became interested in books. In his wonderful world of books he could enjoy the adventures of the story characters and forget his loneliness.

Langston lived in many places while he was growing up. There were many unhappy times in his life. When he was unhappy he would sometimes write down his thoughts in words. These words were written as poems for which he later became very famous.

One summer, while on the train to Mexico to visit his father, Langston was very unhappy and in deep thought. As he crossed the Mississippi River, he began to think of what the old river had meant to Negroes in the past—being sold down the river was the worst thing that could happen to a slave. Thinking of other rivers in the past, such as the Congo, the Niger, and the Nile in Africa, he thought, "I've known rivers." He took an envelope out of his pocket and he wrote a poem called *The Negro Speaks of Rivers.* These verses became one of his most loved poems.

Langston's father offered to send him to college if he would become an engineer. Langston enrolled at Columbia University in New York. He was not interested in his studies and did not like the school. After a year had passed, Langston wrote his father that he could not become an engineer and that he was going to quit school.

Langston had jobs that took him to many places—Africa, Haiti, Russia, Italy, and then back to the United States.

In Washington, D.C. he obtained a job as a bus boy at the Wardman Park Hotel. One day a very famous poet named Vachel Lindsay came to the hotel. That afternoon Langston wrote three of his poems on pieces of paper and put them in his bus boy's coat. In the evening, when Mr. Lindsay came to dinner, Langston laid his poems beside his plate and fearfully departed in haste.

On his way to work next morning, Langston bought a newspaper. As he read it, he was pleasantly shocked to read the headline, VACHEL LINDSAY DISCOVERS NEGRO BUS BOY POET. There were reporters and photographers waiting for him at the hotel. That day was the first time he had ever received so much publicity about his poetry.

From that time on, Langston Hughes became famous not only for his poetry but for his plays, songs, novels, histories and biographies. He is one of the most honored authors in America. He lived in New York City until his death in the spring of 1967.

REMEMBERING LANGSTON HUGHES

A. KNOWING YOUR VOCABULARY

Niger, 119   Haiti, 119

B. THINGS TO REMEMBER

1. Where was Langston born?
2. What did Langston like to do in school?
3. Where did Langston attend college?
4. Who was the famous writer Langston met?
5. When did Langston die?

C. THINGS TO THINK AND TALK ABOUT

1. Langston was often very sad as a child. When he was lonely, he wrote poems. How do you think writing poems made Langston feel better? Have you ever been sad? What do you do when you are sad? What do you like to do when you are happy?
2. When Langston started school, he became involved in a fight and was helped by a white boy. He learned that people are often judged by the color of their skin. Do you have friends from different

races and ethnic groups? What do you learn from them? What do they learn from you?

3. Langston did not want anyone to visit his home when he was poor. Do you think money is important in making friends? Why? Why not? Have you ever heard the expression 'fair weather friends'? What do you think it means?
4. Langston received help from a famous poet in publishing his poetry. Who has helped you accomplish something that you wanted to do? How were you helped and encouraged? Have you ever helped anyone else? How?

D. THINGS TO DO

1. Assemble a display of Langston's books and any available pictures.
2. Read the poem *The Negro Speaks of Rivers*. Arrange an outing to a nearby park or lake. Combine pleasure with an 'on location' creative assignment. Take along writing and drawing materials.

E. BIBLIOGRAPHY

Hughes, Langston. *The First Book of Negroes*. Watts. 1952.

Hughes, Langston. *Famous Negro Heroes of America*. Dodd, Mead. 1964.

Meltzer, Milton. *Langston Hughes, A Biography*. Thomas Y. Crowell Co. 1968.

CHARLES DREW
(1904 - 1950)
Pioneer in Preserving Blood

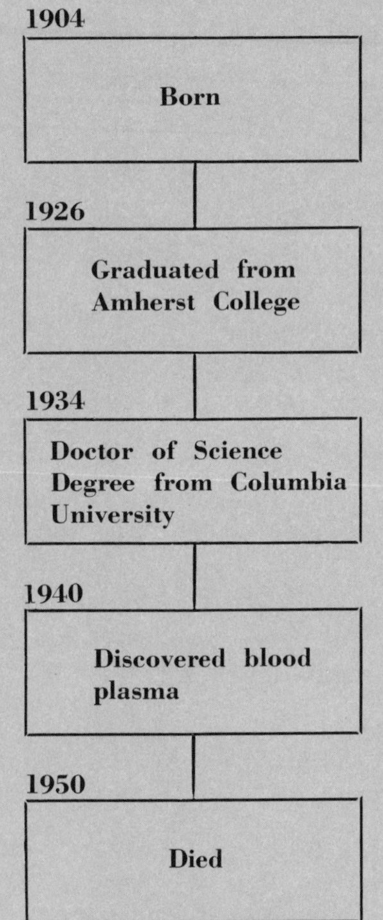

Our most serious crisis (is) the deep division within our society and particularly within our cities - - the divisions between those of our citizens who have never had the opportunity to share in the American dream and those of us who take for granted our jobs, the homes we live in, the education of our children, the family doctor, and the food we eat.

Robert F. Kennedy

MEETING CHARLES DREW

Charles Drew was born in Washington, D.C. When he was a little boy, he liked to swim. He also liked to play baseball and other sports.

His teacher said, "You are good at sports, Charles. You can be a famous football or baseball player."

"I like science," said Charles. "I like to work in the laboratory. I want to become a doctor."

Charles became a doctor and worked at a hospital in New York City. He saw many people die because doctors could not get blood to help them. Charles Drew worked very hard in his laboratory and found a way to keep blood for a long, long time. This blood is called plasma.

In the war, many soldiers' lives were saved because doctors could use blood plasma.

Charles Drew saved many lives. Charles Drew became famous because he had the desire to help people.

KNOWING CHARLES DREW

Charles Drew was born in Washington, on June 3, 1904. He was the son of Richard and Nora Drew. Charles was a very good swimmer by the age of eight. He had also learned to play baseball very well.

He was a good student in high school and a champion athlete. He could have become famous as an athlete but he was more interested in science.

Charles graduated from college in 1926. He was a very good student there and a very good athlete.

After graduation, he taught biology and chemistry at a college in Baltimore, Maryland, for two years. He was also in charge of athletics at the college.

Charles wanted to study medicine and become a doctor. He went to medical school in Montreal, Canada. He continued to be a good student and was still very good in sports. He was such a good worker that he won a fellowship to study more science when he finished at McGill.

Charles then went to work at a hospital in New York City. He was very interested in the study of blood. He worked long hours and finally discovered a way to dry blood so that it could be kept for a long time. This dried blood was called plasma.

Dr. Drew showed the Red Cross how to start the blood bank.

Many soldiers' lives were saved during the war because of this dried blood.

He died in an automobile accident in 1950. The world lost a good friend and a doctor of genius.

UNDERSTANDING CHARLES DREW

Charles Drew was born in Washington, on June 3, 1904. He was the son of Richard and Nora Drew. He showed athletic agility at the age of eight when he became an excellent swimmer. Moreover, he learned to play baseball very well, too.

He was a good student in high school and a champion athlete. He could have become famous as an athlete, but he chose a field of higher interest—science.

Charles was graduated in 1926 from Amherst College where he was a distinguished athlete and student. He received the Howard Hill Mossman Trophy which was awarded annually to the student who contributed the most to various athletics at Amherst during the student's four year college career.

Following graduation, he taught biology and chemistry at Morgan College in Baltimore for two years. Later, he was appointed the Director of Athletics at the college.

Charles had set a great goal for himself, that of studying medicine. He went to McGill Medical School in Montreal, Canada. He continued to excel in scholarship and in sports. As a result, he was elected captain of the McGill track team. Moreover, he was so much in demand as a referee that this job provided extra income for him during his college days.

He did such outstanding work in science that he won membership in the school's medical honorary society. He passed a difficult competitive examination achieving the highest score. His success led to an amount of money for further study.

While at Mc Gill, he heard a lecture on blood and the blood groups. The lecture made Charles think more and more about blood transfusions. And inasmuch as Charles was very interested in blood, the lecturer, Dr. John Beattie, encouraged Charles to do blood research.

The hospital in Montreal set up a laboratory for blood typing in connection with blood transfusions. Charles spent many hours observing doctors' methods. He noticed that doctors spent and lost a great deal of time trying to obtain donors. He thought there should be some way of preserving blood so that it could be available when needed.

Dr. Drew was awarded a two year fellowship in surgery at Presbyterian Hospital in New York City. He worked on experiments which preserved blood over different lengths of time. He started a blood bank with his staff volunteering their blood. Unused blood was discarded after seven days. One day, as a bottle of old blood was about to be discarded, he examined the bottle and reasoned that the plasma had everything except the red cells. He decided that plasma was easy to prepare and that it was necessary to preserve blood over a long period of time. After many hours of hard work and many tests, he found that dried blood could be kept safely for long periods of time.

In 1940, he received his Doctor of Science Degree from Columbia University. His thesis was titled "Banked Blood".

Dr. Drew showed the American Red Cross how to start the blood bank. He became known as "The Father of Blood Plasma." When the war came, many lives were saved because Dr. Charles Drew had found a way to preserve blood plasma. Blood could not be shipped to most parts of the world. Blood plasma is mixed somewhat in the way we mix drinks that come in a package. Only water is needed to make it useable.

Later, Dr. Charles left the blood program and returned to teaching at the university level. In 1950, Charles and some other doctors left Washington for an important meeting of doctors in Atlanta, Georgia. On the way, he fell asleep while driving his car and was killed in the accident. He lay in a field bleeding to death. This great doctor, who had found a way to save lives by having blood on hand, had none when he really needed it.

He was less than 50 years old when he died, but he left his mark on American society. He wanted to help people live and he found a way to help them.

REMEMBERING CHARLES DREW

A. KNOWING YOUR VOCABULARY

science, 124 plasma, 124
competitive, 126 transfusions, 127

B. THINGS TO REMEMBER

1. Where was Charles Drew born?
2. What sports did Charles like to play when he was young?
3. What subjects did Charles study in college?
4. What did Charles do after he graduated from college?
5. How did Dr. Drew help many soldiers during the war?

C. THINGS TO THINK AND TALK ABOUT

1. When Charles was a little boy he liked sports. He was so good at sports that he could have become a professional athlete. Is there more than one occupation that you are interested in? Why is it important to prepare yourself for more than one type of occupation?
2. Charles noticed that many people died because of a lack of blood donors. He decided to do something about it. Is there something in your school

or community that you feel needs changing? What is it? How would you go about changing it?

3. Charles discovered a way of preserving blood. Have you ever thought about discovering something? What?
4. Dr. Drew was known as "The Father of Blood Plasma." Do you know someone who has received a special title because of something they have accomplished? Tell about it.

D. THINGS TO DO

1. Review the life of Charles Drew by writing stories, drawing pictures or discussion.
2. Illustrate a scene from The Life of Dr. Drew.
3. Blood Bank—excellent opportunity to extend understanding of the word 'bank' and the differences between a blood bank and a regular bank.

E. BIBLIOGRAPHY

Hardwick, Richard. *Charles Richard Drew*. Scribners. 1967.

Stratton, Madeline Robinson. *Negroes Who Helped Build America*. Ginn and Company. 1965.

RALPH BUNCHE
(1904 -)
Statesman

1904

Born

1934

PhD in Political Science from Harvard

1941

Authored: "An American Dilemma"

1944

Consultant at the Dumbarton Oaks Conference

1950

Nobel Peace Prize

I wish to say that my peace efforts flowed from the strength of the United Nations.

Dr. Ralph Bunche

MEETING RALPH BUNCHE

When Ralph was eleven years old, his mother died. Not long after that, his father died. Ralph was glad his grandmother was still alive. Ralph went to live with her and they moved to the state of California.

Ralph was a good helper. He sold papers to help make money for his grandmother who was very poor.

He studied hard in school. Most of the boys in his school liked him because he was good in sports.

Grown-up people liked him because he was polite and good to his grandmother. Ralph's friends helped him get enough money to enter college.

Teachers in college knew he was a good worker and had a good mind. They gave him important work to do.

He earned a Doctor's Degree and received very important job assignments working for the government. He became very well known in the United States.

He received many honors including the Nobel Peace Prize.

Ralph worked for the United Nations with people from all over the world.

He wants all people to work together to make our world a good place to live, where all men are good neighbors. To boys and girls he says, "Work hard, be kind, be patient, love everyone no matter who he is and this will be a happy world."

KNOWING RALPH BUNCHE

Ralph Bunche was born in Detroit, Michigan. His father was a barber. The family lived in an apartment over the barber shop. Ralph lived with his father and mother, two aunts, and his grandmother. The family was very poor and Ralph had to work. Ralph had a job selling newspapers.

When he was eleven, his father and mother became sick and died. Ralph and his grandmother moved to Los Angeles, California. Ralph went to elementary school and was a very good student. When he graduated, he won prizes in English and History.

Ralph's grandmother worked very hard as a seamstress in order for Ralph to go to high school. He was very busy while he was in high school. He studied hard. He took part in sports. He worked after school and during the summers to earn money. When Ralph finished high school, he wanted to go to work to help support his grandmother. Grandmother wanted Ralph to enter college. He had been such a good athlete that he won a scholarship to college in Los Angeles, California. Ralph still had to earn money for his books, his clothes, and his food. He worked very hard as a janitor. Ralph won five medals when he was graduated from college in Los Angeles. He won a scholarship to Harvard University. Harvard is a large school in Boston, Massachusettsetts.

Five days before Ralph was to leave for Harvard, his grandmother died. Ralph was very sad. He wanted to stay home but he knew that his grandmother had worked hard all her life so that he could have an education. Ralph left Los Angeles and went to Harvard University because he knew his grandmother would have wanted him to go.

After Ralph graduated from Harvard University, he worked for the government. He helped to write important papers for the United States. He received many honors. One of the honors he received was the Nobel Peace Prize.

Dr. Bunche is now working with the United Nations.

UNDERSTANDING RALPH BUNCHE

Ralph Bunche was born August 7, 1904, in Detroit, Michigan. His father was a barber.

At an early age, Ralph sold newspapers to help with the family income. When Ralph was eleven, both of his parents died.

Ralph's grandmother became the head of the house. She and Ralph moved to Los Angeles and Ralph attended elementary school while his grandmother worked to provide a home for him.

When Ralph graduated from elementary school, he received two prizes. He won prizes in History and English. Ralph was a very good student.

When Ralph was graduated from Jefferson High School in 1922, he received medals for his work in civics and debating.

After graduation, Ralph felt he should go to work to support his grandmother. Grandmother thought otherwise. She wanted Ralph to enter college. Grandmother won the argument. Ralph enrolled at the University of California in Los Angeles, where he received a four year athletic scholarship. In order to earn money to buy textbooks and to have spending money, Ralph applied for a job at the University. He became the gym janitor.

Ralph Bunche was graduated Summa Cum Laude from the University of California at Los Angeles in 1927. He was the Class Valedictorian and he was also elected to Phi Beta Kappa. These were very high honors but Ralph deserved them because of his hard work. He also received five medals for outstanding work and a scholarship for more study at Harvard University.

Ralph's neighbors collected a thousand dollars to help

him with his expenses at Harvard. A few days before he was due to go east to Harvard, his grandmother died. Ralph was very sad and wanted to stay home. He knew, however, that he could best repay his grandmother's hard work and faith in him by continuing his studies. His grandmother would want him to enter Harvard.

Ralph graduated from Harvard in 1928 with a Master of Arts Degree in Political Science. He received many job offers, but finally accepted the opening at Howard University in Washington, D.C. Ralph Bunche was just twenty-four years of age at the time. Ralph enjoyed his work and teaching at Howard University. He married one of his students and the young couple looked forward to a happy future together. Ralph received his assistant professorship and was also appointed assistant to the president of the college. He received another scholarship in 1930 for a year of study at Harvard which enabled him to begin work on his doctorate. In 1931, he received the Rosenwald Fellowship. This fellowship covered his expenses for a year of study and travel in Europe and Africa, doing research for his doctorate on various social problems. He received his doctorate from Harvard in 1934.

In 1936, Ralph was appointed a full professor at Howard University. He was appointed Co-Director of the Institute of Race Relations at Swarthmore College. He was becoming a recognized authority on race relations in the United States. In 1941, he was granted a leave of absence from Howard to tour the United States in order that he might study race relations between people. He worked very hard and wrote extensively. One of the by-products of this tour and study was his book, *An American Dilemma*.

When World War II began, the government requested his services in the Office of Strategic Services. His job was that of researching the areas where the Allies had military interests. When the Allies were ready to plan bases in Africa, Ralph was extremely helpful. He could inform the Allied planners about the traditions, customs, and the attitudes of the people of the area towards the war. He performed his job so well that he became the Associate Chief of the Division of Dependent Territories. Ralph Bunche became the first Afro-American in American history to assume full charge and responsibility for an office in the State Department.

From this point on, he was consultant to many committees and conferences. In particular, many of his suggestions are in the Charter of the United Nations. Everyone recognized that he was a brilliant, hardworking statesman. In 1945, he was a member of the United States delegation to the International Labor Conference in Paris.

In 1946, he was the presidential appointee to the Caribbean Commission in the Virgin Islands. In addition, he attended various United Nations sessions in London and Paris.

Ralph Bunche was asked by the United Nations in 1947 to fly to Palestine to serve as chief aide to the United Nations mediator in trying to establish peace between the Arabs and the Jews. There was much conflict. Moreover, he was often in danger himself. When the United Nations mediator was killed, Ralph Bunche was ordered to take over his duties. For 42 days, he and his staff worked long and hard. Finally, they helped to achieve a temporary peace. Both the Arab. and Jewish leaders praised Ralph Bunche as a great man. Dr. Ralph Bunche was recognized internationally as a peacemaker. As a result, in 1950, he was awarded the Nobel Peace Prize.

From 1950 until 1958, Ralph worked to help the United Nations. He traveled far and wide helping to resolve various explosive situations in the quest for peace. He was in India in 1953 during the Kashmir conflict. In 1955 and 1956, he was in Africa and Egypt trying to maintain peace. He traveled to Ghana in 1958 for the same purpose. In 1959, Dr. Ralph Bunche became the first Afro-American to be nominated as an Overseer at Harvard University.

He returned to Africa in 1960 and, in 1961, was appointed Under-Secretary for Special Political Affairs. This office is one of the top three jobs in the United Nations. While serving in this position Dr. Ralph Bunche made the following statement: "All human beings should act towards one another in a spirit of brotherhood."

Today, Ralph Bunche continues to work for his nation and the world—helping men of all nations to live together in peace and harmony.

REMEMBERING RALPH BUNCHE

A. KNOWING YOUR VOCABULARY

elementary, 132   valedictorian, 134

B. THINGS TO REMEMBER

1. How was Ralph able to attend college?
2. What book did Ralph write?
3. How did Ralph serve his government?
4. What were Ralph's duties with the United Nations?
5. Why is Ralph Bunche called a peace-maker?

C. THINGS TO THINK AND TALK ABOUT

1. When Ralph was a boy, he enjoyed looking at magazines. His father talked to him about the people in the magazines. What magazines are in your home? What magazines do you enjoy most? Who in your family reads to you? Have you learned anything from magazines or books that you think will help you when you are older? Which stories helped you most?
2. After Ralph's parents died, his grandmother took care of him. Do you have a grandmother or other relative whom you love very much? What do they do that indicates that they also love you very much?
3. Ralph's grandmother was determined that Ralph enter college. He worked hard to help pay for his education. Is there anyone who is encouraging you to work hard in school? What do they say to you? What do you think you will do to help pay for your education?
4. Ralph became ill while he was in college. He missed one year of school but still managed to

graduate with high honors. Have you ever missed school because of a long illness? How did you manage to catch up with your work? If some-one returned to our class after a long absence, what do you think we could do to help?

5. Dr. Bunche received the Nobel prize for his work with the United Nations. Dr. Bunche dreamed of a world in which people lived together in peace. What are your thoughts about world peace? How do you think people could live together in peace?

D. THINGS TO DO

1. Explore the meaning of the word PEACE. Write a chart story on 'What Peace Means to Us'.
2. Research and discuss the following abbreviations: B.A., M.A., M.D., Ed.D. Ph.D., LL.D.
3. Stage a mock U.N. Assembly. Assign children to serve as delegates from different countries. Ask each delegate to deliver a speech on PEACE.

E. BIBLIOGRAPHY

Kugehmass, J. Alvin. *Ralph J. Bunche: Fighter for Peace*. Messner. 1962.

Sechrist, Elizabeth. *Its Times for Brotherhood*. Mac-rae and Smith & Co. 1962.

Shapp, Martha and Charles. *Lets Find Out About the United Nations*. Franklin Watts, Inc. 1963.

MARIAN ANDERSON
(1908 -)
Concert Singer

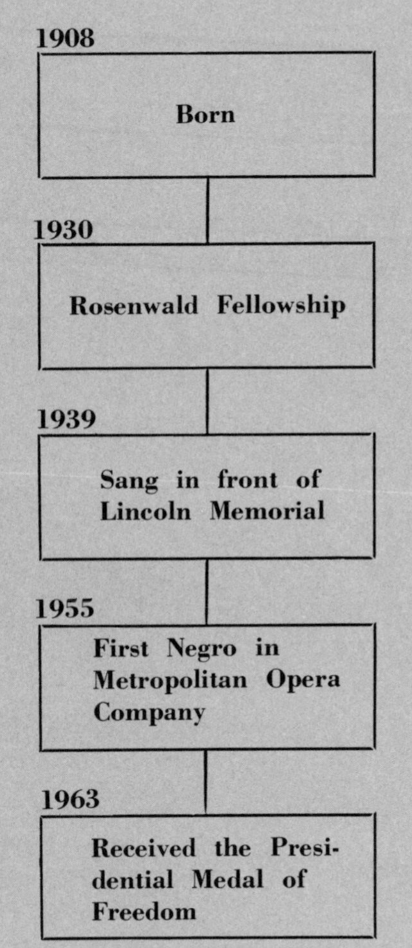

Let a new earth rise. Let another world be born. Let a bloody peace be written in the sky. Let a second generation full of courage issue forth; let a people loving freedom come to growth.

Margaret Walker
For My People

MEETING MARIAN ANDERSON

Marian loved singing and she loved music. She would sing anytime anyone asked her to sing.

She worked very hard to buy a violin for $3.00. Her father saw how much she loved music so he saved and bought a second-hand piano for her.

Marian sang in the church choir. She loved to sing so much that she took singing lessons. One day, when she was seventeen years old, her music teacher said to her, "There is a singing contest in a big city. I will take you there because I think you will win." There were 300 singers in the contest. Marian won first prize. Everyone was very proud of her.

Marian sang all over the world. She sang for kings and queens and presidents. She sang for the rich. She sang for the poor.

When she became very famous, she stood in front of the big Lincoln Memorial in Washington, D.C., and sang for 75,000 people.

KNOWING MARIAN ANDERSON

It was a big day in the Anderson home in Philadelphia. The family had saved enough money to buy a second-hand piano. The three Anderson girls, Marian, Alice, and Ethel, were having fun playing notes on the piano with their father. The girls knew that their father was a wonderful man. He was a church-going man and very popular. Their mother was gay and the family enjoyed many happy times together.

The piano would be very nice for the oldest daughter, Marian, who was eight years old. She loved music and had already saved $3.00 to buy a violin. She was a member of the church choir at the Union Baptist Church. Even when she was little, she sang all by herself in front of the church members.

Soon after they got the piano, Marian's father died. Mrs. Anderson worked in a store so that she could make money for the family. One Saturday Mrs. Anderson was at home working and some church ladies came to the house. They said, "Your daughter, Marian, has such a lovely voice that we have collected money for her so that she can take singing lessons." The Andersons thought the ladies were very kind. Later, other friends and even school children collected money so that Marian could have lessons for her beautiful voice.

When she was seventeen years old, her singing teacher said, "Now you are ready to enter a big singing contest in New York City. The winner will be the new singer for a huge orchestra." Marian entered and won.

Marian became famous and traveled throughout the world. She sang for kings, queens and presidents. She sang for the rich and the poor. She sang for everyone.

When she became very famous, she stood in front of the big Lincoln Memorial in Washington, D.C., and sang for 75,000 people.

Marian Anderson was the first Afro-American to acquire a regular job as a singer in the Metropolitan Opera House. She sang many songs on that famous stage and wore many lovely costumes.

Marian Anderson sang for over fifty years. She has retired from singing so that she can spend more time on her big farm.

UNDERSTANDING MARIAN ANDERSON

Marian Anderson was born in Philadelphia, Pennsylvania, on February 27, 1908. Marian was the oldest of three sisters. Her two younger sisters were named Alice and Ethel. Her father was a hard working man. He was also an usher at the Union Baptist Church. The entire family went to church every Sunday.

By the time Marian was eight, she was singing in the Sunday School Choir and possessed a wonderful voice. One day, Marian was walking down the street when she saw a violin in a store window. The price tag read $3.49. Marian wanted the violin. She began to save all the pennies, nickles, and dimes that she could earn. When she had $3.00, she returned to the store and asked the man if she could have the violin and owe him $.49. The owner agreed and Marian proudly took the violin home. She played the violin until her father bought a secondhand piano. She left her violin to play the piano. The piano became her first love because she could play and sing at the same time. When Marian's father died, her mother had to work in a dry goods store to support her family.

Marian continued to sing at church and at local clubs and societies. She became well-known around Philadelphia. When she was fourteen, she joined the senior choir at the Union Baptist Church. She was so eager to sing that she learned all four voice parts of each hymn so that she could sing any part in which she might be needed.

When Marian was 17, she was entered by her music teacher in the New York Philharmonic Competition. There were over 300 singers entered in the competition and Marian thought she had little chance of winning. Imagine her surprise when she was announced the winner!

She returned to Philadelphia and continued singing and giving concerts. However, she received little money for the concerts.

Marian was awarded a Rosenwald Fellowship in 1930 which gave her the money for a year of study in Europe. She made her debut in Paris and was awarded great honors. Everyone thought she had a wonderful voice.

Marian returned to the United States and continued to give concerts. The audiences thought she had a great voice but she still received little money.

Marian returned to Europe in 1933. In one year's time she gave 142 concerts in Norway, Sweden, Denmark and Finland. She was acclaimed as a great singer in these countries and was received by kings and queens.

In 1934, she made her debut in Berlin to wild applause. Everyone wanted to hear this great singer. In 1935, she made her debut in Austria. She sang to large audiences who thought she was the world's greatest singer.

Upon her return to the United States, she was greeted as a great success. She continued to give concerts in the United States and South America. She was honored everywhere.

Marian sang on the steps of the Lincoln Memorial in Washington, D.C. She was introduced by the Secretary of the Interior. There were 75,000 people listening to her at the Memorial while millions listened to her on their radio at home. Everyone agreed that she was the world's greatest singer. She was awarded the Spingarn Award by the NAACP as a great American.

In 1955, Marian was signed to sing for the Metropolitan Opera Company. She was the first Afro-American selected to sing a major role for the company.

She continued to give concerts around the world. In 1963, she also received the Presidential Medal of Freedom.

In 1965, she was elected to the Women's Hall of Fame. She announced that she was going to retire from the concert stage at the year's end. She completed a world tour and ended with a final concert at Carnegie Hall. Her performance was so outstanding that the audience continued to applaud long after she left the stage. She responded by performing another hour. When she left the stage, applause could be heard for thirty more minutes. What a fitting tribute to a great singer!

REMEMBERING MARIAN ANDERSON

A. KNOWING YOUR VOCABULARY
   choir, 141   Metropolitan Opera, 143

B. THINGS TO REMEMBER
   1. When did Marian begin singing?
   2. Why was it an honor for Marian to sing with the Metropolitan Opera Company?
   3. What did Marian do in 1963?
   4. What honor did Marian receive in 1965?
   5. How did Marian help the cause of civil rights?

C. THINGS TO THINK AND TALK ABOUT
   1. Marian Anderson was a great singer. She also played the violin. Do you know anyone who has a special talent in music? Do you have any special talent in music? If you could take instrumental lessons, what instrument would you prefer to play?
   2. Marian won a singing contest. She ranked first among three hundred contestants. What do you think her thoughts were at that moment? Have you ever taken part in a contest? Did you win or lose? How do you feel when you win? How do you feel when you lose?
   3. Marian was refused the opportunity to sing for a certain organization because she was a Negro.

She performed instead on the steps of the Lincoln Memorial. Why do you think she chose that place to give her concert?

D. THINGS TO DO

1. Learn and sing patriotic songs such as 'America' which Marian sang on the steps of the Lincoln Memorial.
2. Write about other famous Afro-Americans in music: Leontyne Price, Mahalia Jackson, William Warfield, Sammy Davis Jr., etc.
3. Visit a nearby church and choir loft. Plan the visit when the organist can be present to give a demonstration and answer questions about the organ.

E. BIBLIOGRAPHY

Hughes, Langston. *Famous Negro Music Makers*. Dodd Mead. 1955.

Newman, Shirlee. *Marian Anderson*. Westminister. 1966.

JACK ROOSEVELT ROBINSON
(1919 -   )
First Negro Baseball Player In the Major Leagues

1919

Born

1947

Signed to play with the Dodgers

1949

Named Most Valuable Player in the National League

1962

Elected to Baseball's Hall of Fame

1967

Entered business and social welfare

This nation was founded by men of many nations and backgrounds. It was founded on the principle that all men are created equal, and that the rights of every man are diminished when the rights of one man are threatened.

John F. Kennedy

MEETING JACKIE ROBINSON

Jackie loved his older brother Mack. "Mack is a great athlete," said Jackie. "I want to be just like him."

Jackie went out for football and became a star just like his brother had been. He went out for the basketball, baseball, and track teams, too.

When it came time for college, Jackie went out for the football, basketball, and track team. Moreover, he wanted to become a physical education teacher because he liked sports so much.

He had to leave school when his uncle became sick because his mother had to stop working to take care of him and could not give Jackie money for books. When the war came, Jackie joined the army.

After his army duty, Jackie taught physical education for a short time. Then he played baseball for a living. He made more money playing baseball so he went on playing because he knew he could help his mother and his uncle. Jackie Robinson played baseball for many years and became the first Afro-American to play in the major leagues.

One day, his brother Mack came to see him play in New York City. Mack watched Jackie steal two bases in the game. He said, "My brother always loved to run. When he was little he used to run with me. I always beat him, but I don't think I could beat him now."

KNOWING JACKIE ROBINSON

Jack Roosevelt Robinson was born in Cairo, Georgia. He was the youngest of five children. Jack's father died when he was about a year old. Soon after his father died, Jack's mother moved to California with all her children. She found a job and worked hard to send Jack and his brothers and sister to school. Mack was Jack's oldest brother. Jack loved Mack and wanted to be just like him.

In high school, Mack became a champion runner and broad jumper. Jack decided he would try out for sports, too. When Jack entered high school, he followed in Mack's footsteps and became a star athlete. He played football, basketball, and baseball. He also joined the track team. When Jack entered college, he continued his outstanding athletic record. He wanted to become a physical education teacher. He went out for football and became a star in his first year by setting a new record in college football.

During the Second World War, Jack served as a second lieutenant in the Army. After the war, he played short-stop for the Kansas City Monarchs, a team in the Negro American Baseball league. Many scouts watched Jack play baseball. He was finally talked into playing major league baseball. Jackie Robinson became the first Afro-American to play in the major leagues. Jackie was named Rookie of the Year in 1947. He was named the Most Valuable Player in 1949.

In 1957, Jackie retired from major league baseball. Jackie Robinson had paved the way for other Afro-Americans to play in major league baseball.

UNDERSTANDING JACKIE ROBINSON

Jack Roosevelt Robinson was born on January 31, 1919, in Cairo, Georgia. He was the youngest of five children. Jack's father died when he was still a baby.

When Jack was about fourteen months old, Mrs. Mallie Robinson moved to Pasadena, California with all of her children. Her brother, Burton welcomed his sister, the four boys and one girl whose ages ranged from fourteen months to ten years.

Mrs. Robinson had a part-time job as a domestic servant and did her best to keep the children clean, well-fed, and in school. Uncle Burton helped as much as he could and became almost like a second father to the five children.

The children attended Cleveland Elementary School and then enrolled at Muir Technical High School. Mack was Jackie's oldest brother and was Jackie's hero. Mack became a champion runner and a broad jumper in high school. Jackie entered sports in elementary school.

When Jackie was fourteen, he entered high school and followed in his brother Mack's footsteps. He became a star athlete. He played on the football, basketball, baseball, and track teams.

Jack's brother, Mack, was a U.S. contestant in the Berlin Olympics of 1936 and finished the 200 meter dash second to Jesse Owens. Jack still wanted to be like Mack. When he entered Pasadena Junior College in 1936, he continued with his outstanding athletic record. He set a new junior college broad jump record of 25 feet 6½ inches. He led the Junior College Conference in baseball with a batting average of .460 and, in one basketball game, he scored 28 points. In the beginning of his second year Jackie was almost 6 feet tall and weighed 175 pounds. He was a very popular student and not at all conceited. He was noted for his fair sportsmanship.

Jackie finished Pasadena Junior College in 1939 and then registered at the University of California at Los Angeles. He wanted to major in physical education. He immediately went out for football and became a star in his first year. However he received a sprained ankle near the end of the season, but he had set a new record in college football. Jackie had carried the ball 14 times for an average of 20 yards gained per carry. Jackie's name first became well known in the world of sports because he was an exceptional football star.

Jackie was also a star in basketball and in track. In basketball he started in twelve games and became the top scorer. He also broke the broad jump record in track.

Jackie hoped to marry Rachel Isum, a girl he had met in college, but his Uncle Burton became ill and Jackie was needed at home to help with the work. He quit college in his last year and worked at a Civilian Conservation Corps camp as an athletic director.

When the camp closed, an offer came for Jackie to play in the All-Star Charity Football Game in Chicago. As a result of this game, he was selected by the Los Angeles Bulldogs to play in professional football. He played until December 7, 1941. On this day the Japanese attacked Pearl Harbor. Jackie enlisted in the army and was sent to Fort Riley, Texas, for his basic training. He met the famous Afro-American boxer Joe Louis at Fort Riley, and the two men became good friends. When his basic training was completed, Joe Louis suggested that Jackie apply for Officers' Candidate School. Jackie applied and was accepted. He was sent to the 761st Tank Battalion at Camp Hood, Texas. Jackie's bad ankle began to bother him there, so after 31 months of army duty, Jackie was honorably discharged from the service.

Jackie returned to Pasadena after his army service. His mother's former pastor was now the president of a small Negro college, in Austin, Texas. The president offered Jackie the position of athletic director. Jackie accepted the job because he liked working with young people. He only stayed a short period because the salary was very low. Moreover, Jackie's Uncle Burton was bed-ridden and Jackie's mother could not work and leave him alone.

Jackie received an offer to play shortstop from the Kansas City Monarchs, a team in the Negro American Baseball League. The salary was good and Jackie accepted the offer. He went on the road with the team and it was hard work, but Jackie could send money home and still have enough to get married.

Jackie and Rachel Isum, his college sweetheart, were married in 1946.

Many baseball scouts watched Jackie playing for the Monarchs and he was finally persuaded to travel to New York City and talk with Branch Rickey of the Brooklyn Dodgers about playing in the major leagues.

Jackie was sent to the Dodgers' International League Club in Montreal, Canada. Jackie switched from shortstop to second base. He played sensational ball the entire year. The Montreal team won the pennant that year as well as the Little World Series. Jackie led the league with a batting average of .349. He also led the league with 155 hits and 113 runs scored.

Although Jackie led the International League in batting and was an outstanding player, there were many people who felt that he should not be brought up to the major leagues. These people felt that a Negro had no place in baseball. Branch Rickey felt otherwise. On April 10, 1947, he signed Jackie Robinson as a member of the Dodgers.

The first year was very difficult for Jackie. He had to hold his temper and let his brilliant baseball playing answer the unfairness of some of the other players. Jackie played such good ball that he helped his team win the pennant. He was named Rookie of the Year in 1947. Two years later, in 1949, Jackie was named the Most Valuable Player in the National League. He was batting champion in 1949, with a batting average of .342. Jackie continued playing baseball for another eight years and was always a good player. He was exceptionally good at stealing bases, particularly home base. His playing heightened the excitement of the game because the fans always hoped to see Jackie steal a base.

Jackie retired from baseball in 1957 to become vice president of a big company in New York City. However, Jackie had paved the way for other all-star Afro-Americans to play in the major leagues!

REMEMBERING JACKIE ROBINSON

A. KNOWING YOUR VOCABULARY

champion, 150 contestant, 152
conceited, 152 athletic, 152

B. THINGS TO REMEMBER

1. Why did Jackie admire his brother Mack?
2. What sports did Jackie participate in when he was in high school?
3. How did Jackie begin playing with the Dodgers?
4. Why did Jackie experience difficulty playing in the Major Leagues?
5. How did Jackie heighten the excitement of a baseball game?

C. THINGS TO THINK AND TALK ABOUT

1. Jackie wanted to be just like his brother Mack. Whom do you know in your family or school that you would like to imitate? Why?
2. Jackie wanted to become a physical education teacher. How many different types of teachers do you know? What kind of teacher would you like to be? Why?
3. When Jackie entered high school, he participated in many different sports. What is your favorite sport? Would you like to make a career of your favorite sport? What is the difference between a career and a hobby?
4. Jackie was forced to leave school for a time in order to help his family. Have you ever had to go without something in order to help someone in your family? Has anyone in your family ever gone without something in order to help you? Tell us about it.

5. After Jackie's father died, his uncle Burton became like a second father to him. Do you have any relatives other than your parents who are very special to you? Who are they? Why do you love them so much?

D. THINGS TO DO

1. Collect and display pictures of other baseball players. Identify players with teams and positions.
2. Describe the position of each player on a baseball team.
3. Define the following baseball terms:

runs	strike	fly
outs	bunt	homer
shortstop	pitcher	innings
umpire	mound	catcher
grounder	pop-up	fielder
steal bases	dugout	foul
error	diamond	batter up

E. BIBLIOGRAPHY

Robinson, Jackie and Duckett, Alfred. *Breakthrough To the Big League: The Story of Jackie Robinson.* Harper and Row. 1965.

Shapiro, Milton J. *Jackie Robinson of the Brooklyn Dodgers*. Messner. 1957.

MARTIN LUTHER KING JR.
(1929 - 1968)
Fighter for Peace and Freedom

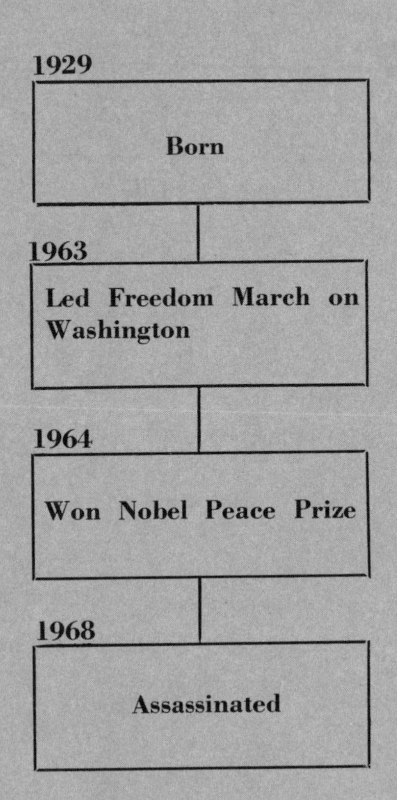

All humanity is involved in a single process, and all men are brothers. To the degree that I harm my brother, no matter what he is doing to me, to that extent I am harming myself. Why is this? Because men are brothers. If you harm me, you harm yourself.

Dr. Martin Luther King, Jr.

MEETING MARTIN LUTHER KING, JR.

One day, when he was about 7 years old, Martin Luther King, Jr. said to his mother, "When I grow up, I want to be like my father. I want to help people. Maybe I will be a minister like my father."

"Your father works very hard," said Martin's mother. "You will have to work very hard, also."

When Martin was little he was a very good student. He finished high school when he was only fifteen years old.

By the time Martin had finished college he was sure he wanted to be a minister like his father. He went to another college to study for the ministry. When he graduated, he was appointed minister of a church in Alabama.

In the city where Martin worked, Afro-Americans almost always rode in the back of buses. The front part of the bus was usually reserved for white people. A Negro woman was put in jail one day because she would not ride in the back of the bus. Martin visited the woman in jail. They talked for a long, long time. Martin did not think it was right for Afro-Americans to be forced to ride in the back of any bus.

Martin discussed the problem with other Negro leaders of the city. They decided not to ride the buses. Most of the Negroes in the city stopped riding the buses. At the end of a year, the law was changed. Now Afro-Americans can sit in the back or in the front of the bus.

Martin Luther King, Jr. and the other black Americans had won a big fight by using peaceful means.

KNOWING MARTIN LUTHER KING, JR.

Martin Luther King, Jr. was born in Atlanta, Georgia. Martin's father was pastor of a church in Atlanta. Martin spent much time in his father's church listening to his father preach. He learned what it meant to help people.

Martin could not decide what he wanted to be when he grew up. His mother wanted him to be a doctor. His father wanted him to be a minister. Martin finally decided to be a minister—a minister who would lead his people to freedom.

While Martin was at college, he learned about a great man from India who had freed his people by peaceful means. Martin never forgot what he had learned about peaceful ways of winning a fight. When Reverend King finished college, he returned to Montgomery, Alabama, and became the pastor of a church.

Soon after Dr. King began working, a Negro lady was arrested and put in jail because she would not move to the back of the bus. Negroes were supposed to ride in the back of the bus. Usually, only white people could sit in the front of the bus.

Dr. King met with other Afro-American leaders. In protest, they decided not to ride the buses. The next morning almost every Negro in Montgomery, Alabama, stopped riding the buses. Some black people had to walk four or five miles to work because they did not want to ride in the back of the bus. They did this because they believed they were right.

After a year, the court ruled that Negroes could sit anywhere they wished in the city buses. This change in the law was a big victory for Afro-Americans.

In August of 1963, Martin Luther King, Jr. led a big "Freedom March" in Washington, D.C. Thousands of people marched to the Lincoln Memorial. Most people marched peacefully.

Martin Luther King, Jr. received his biggest honor in 1964. He won the Nobel Peace Prize. He used the money from the prize to help the cause of black Americans.

He was an important leader of his people until he was assassinated on April 4, 1968, in Memphis, Tennessee.

UNDERSTANDING MARTIN LUTHER KING, JR.

Martin Luther King Jr. was born on January 15, 1929, in his grandmother's house in Atlanta, Georgia.

Martin's father was the pastor of a church, and when Martin, Jr. was young, his second home was the church. He heard his father preach and was taught what it meant to "turn the other cheek."

Martin received good grades in school and spoke so well that he won many contests for public speaking.

As Martin grew older, he had a choice to make. His father thought Martin Jr. should follow in his footsteps and become a minister. A book helped Martin Jr. make his choice. The book described "civil disobedience"—not obeying laws that allowed the abuse and mistreatment of people.

Martin knew that if "civil disobedience" were to be effective, many people would have to hear about it. Martin Jr. decided to be a minister—a minister who would lead his people to freedom. After Martin Jr. finished his studies, he was ordained a minister and elected assistant pastor of Ebenezer Baptist Church, where his father had served for many years. Dr. King Jr. wanted to learn more, so he went to Crozer Theological Seminary. Reverend King learned at Crozer about Mohandas K. Gandhi of India who had freed his people with non-violent, peaceful methods. After Reverend King was graduated from Crozer, he studied at Boston University for his doctorate, one of the highest degrees in education.

While Reverend King was in Boston, he met Coretta Scott. He fell in love with her and they were married. When Reverend King finished studying in Boston, he returned to Alabama with his wife to serve as pastor of the Dexter Avenue Baptist Church in Montgomery.

Soon after Reverend King began working Mrs. Rosa Parks was arrested and put in jail because she would not move to the back of the bus. Black Americans were supposed to ride in the back of public transportation vehicles. When Reverend King and the other Negro leaders heard of Mrs. Parks' arrest, they planned an act of "civil disobedience." They decided to boycott the buses. On the following morning, almost every Afro-American who usually rode the bus walked to work or drove a car.

The Negroes of Montgomery, Alabama, continued this boycott—protest—for one year. Finally, the United States Supreme Court ruled that Alabama's bus segregation law was unconstitutional. This means that the law went against the laws of the United States Constitution. Thus, it was illegal.

This revision of law was a genuine triumph for Afro-Americans. Because they had fought together—peacefully—they had won the respect of the world for their victory.

Dr. King formed a new organization called the Southern Christian Leadership Conference.

The people staged sit-ins, marches, and demonstrations to publicize this fight for freedom to the people of the world.

One of the biggest freedom marches was held on August 28, 1963. It was called the March on Washington. Thousands of people gathered, and together they marched to the Lincoln Memorial. Reverend King led the march. There was no violence. Everyone marched peacefully. This march gave the Civil Rights movement new importance and Congress began to take interest in the Civil Rights Bill that President Kennedy had proposed.

On October 14, 1964, Martin Luther King, Jr. received his biggest honor. He was awarded the Nobel Peace Prize. Reverend King was the youngest man to receive this prize of $54,000. He donated the money to the

Civil Rights movement.

Dr. Martin Luther King, Jr. was mortally wounded by an assassin's bullet on April 4, 1968 in Memphis, Tennessee. Dr. King was in Memphis to demonstrate nonviolently for the cause of those ideals which he so long had held to be inviolable. His death shall not alter the long road he has traveled. There will be many who will live by his ideas and beliefs and will continue to follow and practice his philosophy of nonviolence.

REMEMBERING MARTIN LUTHER KING

A. KNOWING YOUR VOCABULARY

reserved, 159   protest, 160
segregation, 163   demonstrations, 163

B. THINGS TO REMEMBER

1. Who did Martin want to resemble when he grew up?
2. What is a boycott?
3. How did Martin and his people use the boycott?
4. What award did Martin receive in 1964?
5. What did Martin do with the money he received?

C. THINGS TO THINK AND TALK ABOUT

1. When Martin was a boy, he wanted to be like his father. Is there someone in your family, in your school, or in your city whom you admire? Is there someone whom you would like to resemble?
2. Martin studied in college for the ministry. A minister must be able to speak well. Why? Do you like to speak? Why is it important for you to learn how to speak well? What jobs can you think of that require people who can speak especially well?
3. Martin helped to change a law. What is the dif-

ference between a law and a rule? Are there any rules in your home or in your school that you think should be altered or abolished? How could you bring about change in a peaceful way?

4. While Martin was at school, he learned about a great man from India who helped his people by peaceful means. What ways do you know of solving problems peacefully? Must disagreements always involve fighting or injuring someone?
5. When the Negroes refused to ride the buses in Alabama, they were forced to walk many miles to work. They did not mind the inconvenience because they were trying to change a law that they thought was junjust. Have you ever had to go without something or had to work very hard to prove that you were right? When?

D. THINGS TO DO

1. Display photographs and available pictures such as the march on Washington. Attach mural paper to the length of the chalkboard.
2. Debate violence vs. non-violence.

E. BIBLIOGRAPHY

King, Martin Luther. *A Martin Luther King Treasury*. Educational Treasury. 1964.

King, Martin Luther. *Why We Can't Wait*. Harper & Row. 1963-1964.

King, Martin Luther. *Where Do We Go From Here: Chaos or Community?* Harper & Row. 1967.

WILLIE HOWARD MAYS
(1931-   )
Baseball Player

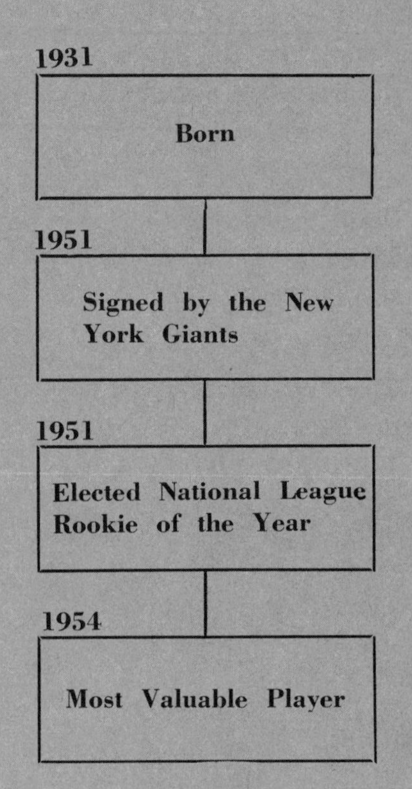

The real hero of this struggle is the American Negro. His actions and protest, his courage to risk safety and even to risk his life, have awakened the conscience of this nation. His demonstrations have been designed to call attention to injustice, designed to provoke change, designed to stir reform. He has called upon us to make good the promise of America. And who among us can say that we would have the same progress were it not for his persistent bravery, and his faith in American democracy.

Lyndon B. Johnson

MEETING WILLIE HOWARD MAYS

"Let's go to the movies," Johnny said to Willie.

"No," said Willie, "I want to play ball!"

"Oh, you always want to play ball." Johnny said.

"Sure, I do! Someday, maybe I'll be like Babe Ruth. He is a great ball player. Everyone knows him."

Willie went into his house. His father was reading.

"Dad, all the kids have gone to the movies. Will you come out and throw a few balls to me?"

"Sure," said his father.

They played ball many nights before supper.

One day Johnny told Willie that he was going to move far away.

"Good bye," said Willie.

"Good bye," said Johnny. "Always remember me. Let's write to each other."

Willie Mays grew up and went to high school. He played on the baseball team. Most of his friends liked to watch him bat. He hit many home runs.

A few years later, when Johnny was reading the paper, he saw a picture of a baseball player.

"Look," he said to his father, "that is Willie Mays. He plays with the San Francisco Giants. I remember when we were boys and he lived in our neighborhood."

"Yes, I remember, too. He always wanted to play baseball.

"Let's watch the game on T.V. today. Maybe I'll see my friend hit a home run."

KNOWING WILLIE HOWARD MAYS

Willie Howard Mays was born in Westfield, Alabama. He was raised by his Aunt Sarah. She was his father's sister. Willie's father worked in a steel mill. He worked very hard but he still had time to play baseball with Willie.

He played baseball with his son from the time Willie could roll a ball. When he had no one with whom to play, he would go to a field and throw a ball in the air and bat it as hard as he could. He would run around the bases as fast as he could and slide across home plate. He would get up, brush the dust off, go find his ball, and hit it again and again.

When Willie was sixteen years old, he was such a good ball player that a baseball team called "The Birmingham Barons" paid him to play center field. Willie was surprised when he found out he was going to be paid for playing baseball. "Baseball is fun," he said. "I would play for nothing."

Because Willie could hit the ball far and run fast he was signed to play with the Giants. The Giants are one of the major league teams. Willie hit his first major league home run in the Giant's ball park. He has hit over 525 major league home runs.

GIANTS
GIANTS

UNDERSTANDING WILLIE HOWARD MAYS

Willie Howard Mays was born in Westfield, Alabama, on May 6, 1931. Westfield was a suburb of Birmingham. His parents were Ann and Howard, but they were divorced when Willie was about five years old. Willie went to live with his Aunt Sarah, his father's sister. Aunt Sarah lived in Fairfield, which was a larger suburb of Birmingham, and it was there that Willie grew up. Before we go further, be sure that you know our man's name is Willie and not William. His name was not a nickname for William.

Willie's father worked in a nearby steel mill. He worked hard in the mill's tool room. He also played semi-professional baseball. He played baseball with his son from the time Willie could roll a ball. At three years of age, Willie was playing catch on a baseball diamond with his father.

By the time he was six years of age, Willie was playing baseball. He would go to a field, lay out three bases, and pick a home plate. Then he would throw a ball and bat it as hard as he could. Rather than get the ball, he would run around the bases as fast as he could and end up by sliding across home plate. He would get up, brush the dust off, go find his ball, and then hit it again and again. Sometimes his best friend, Charley, would play catch with him. Charley would hit the ball and Willie would chase it.

When Willie's father saw how interested Willie was in baseball, he would play with him. He would hit ground balls to Willie, and Willie would chase after them and then throw them back to his father from anywhere on the field. Willie loved to play this game with his father.

When Willie was ten, he was a big and very healthy boy. He played baseball with boys who were four or five years older than he was. He loved baseball, but he also liked basketball and football. Perhaps his interest in baseball was helped by his father's great interest in the game. By the time Willie was fourteen, he was playing on the same team as his father.

All this time Willie was attending school where he was a very good student. He attended the Fairfield Industrial School, and his principal and athletic coach both urged him to plan on attending college. His father wanted Willie to do well in school because he did not want him to work in a steel mill.

At the age of 16, Willie was playing professional ball with the Birmingham Barons in the Negro Semi-Pro League. He became a utility outfielder. Because he was playing for money, he could not play for his school teams. However, he kept up his marks and graduated with his class. When Willie joined the Barons and learned that he would be paid $300.00 for playing baseball, he was amazed. He said, "Baseball is fun. I would play for nothing."

During the first summer that Willie was playing for the Barons, the regular centerfielder was hurt. Willie went in as a substitute. Willie was the regular centerfielder from that time on.

In the following year, Willie got his big league chance by accident. One of the Giants' farm clubs needed a first baseman. They heard that there was a good first baseman playing with the Birmingham Barons, Willie's team. A scout was went to watch the team play. The scout found the first baseman to be a good player, but he was too old. However, the scout did see a seventeen year old centerfielder who was a good player. He could catch fly balls. He could hit. He could run very fast. He was a good baseball player, and he was only seventeen. The scout promptly signed Willie to a contract with the New York Giants.

Willie was sent to Trenton, which was in the Interstate League. He played in 81 games and batted .353.

He played 35 games for Minneapolis of the American Association. He batted .477. He liked Minneapolis and Minneapolis liked him. There was not much happiness one June night when Willie was called up to play with the New York Giants. He joined the team in Philadelphia where he played two games in centerfield but did not get a hit when he was at bat. He waited until he was back at the Polo Grounds, the home of the Giants, to get his first hit. He hit a home run over the left field roof. He played so well for the Giants in 1951 that he was elected National League Rookie of the Year.

In 1952, Willie only played 34 games for the Giants. He enlisted in the Army. He served for the remainder of 1952 and all of the 1953 season. He returned to the Giants in 1954 and led the league in hitting. Upon his return, he hit a home run in his first game.

Willie is one of the great figures in baseball today. He will probably be one of the great figures in all-time baseball. He is second only to Babe Ruth in total home runs. He has broken many, many records.

One night, in 1961, Willie matched a record in Milwaukee that made him very happy. He stepped up to bat and hit a home run. The next time up he hit a long fly ball that was caught at the fence in center field. In the next two times up, Willie hit home runs. When he came up to bat in the 9th inning, he thought about the other eight men who had hit four home runs in one game. The pitch came, Willie hit it and he had another RUN—four homers in one game. He was so happy that he jumped around the bases.

All of his training from an early age has made Willie Mays a great centerfielder for the Giants. Will is 5' 10¼" tall and weights about 180 pounds. He throws and bats right handed.

Willie has received many honors while playing baseball. Some of them are:

1951 - National League Rookie of the Year.
1954 - National League's Most Valuable Player.
1955 - Led the National League in home runs—51.
1956 - Led the National League for stolen bases—40.
1957 - Led the National League for stolen bases—38.
1958 - Led the National League for stolen bases—31.
1959 - Led the National League for stolen bases—27.
1960 - Led the National League for stolen bases—25.
1962 - Led the National League with the most home runs—49.
1964 - Led the National League with the most home runs—47.
1965 - Led the National League with the most home runs—52.
1965 - National Leagues's Most Valuable Player.

REMEMBERING WILLIE MAYS

A. KNOWING YOUR VOCABULARY

league, 168 contract, 172

B. THINGS TO REMEMBER

1. What game did Willie enjoy playing when he was very young?
2. Who worked very hard but still had time to play with Willie?
3. What did Willie do when he had to play alone?
4. How did Willie acquire his contract with the New York Giants?
5. What contributions did Willie make to the game of baseball?

C. THINGS TO THINK AND TALK ABOUT

1. Willie was interested in baseball from the time he was a child. He liked to play baseball with his friends. What games do you like to play with your friends? What does it mean to be 'a good sport'? Are you a good sport? How do you know?
2. Willie's father encouraged his interest by playing ball with him. Who in your family plays with you? Who in your family encourages you in your interests? What does your family think you will be when you grow up? What do you think you will be?
3. After Willie became famous, his friend Johnny saw his picture in the newspaper. Have you ever known anyone whose picture appeared in the newspaper? Tell us about it.
4. Willie invented a way to play baseball by himself. What games can you play alone? What games need more than one player? Have you ever invented a

game? Describe it.

5. Willie was surprised when he learned that he would be paid for playing baseball. He considered baseball fun—not work. Have you ever received pay for anything? Was it work or fun? Is there something that you would like to do when you grow up that seems more fun than work?

D. THINGS TO DO

1. Write a biography about Willie Mays.
2. Collect pictures or draw a picture of Willie Mays playing baseball when he was young and when he grew older.

E. BIBLIOGRAPHY

Hano, Arnold. *Willie Mays*. Grosset and Dunlap. 1966.
Pratt, J. Lowell. *Baseball's All Stars.* Doubleday. 1967.
Shapiro, Milton J. *The Willie Mays Story*. Massner & Company. 1960.

Afro-American Landmarks and Milestones

1492 Negro servants, slaves, and explorers came to the New World with the first Spanish and French explorers. Pedro Alonso Nino of Columbus' crew is identified as a Negro by some scholars.

1513 Balboa's expedition to the Pacific included 30 Negroes who were instrumental in clearing the way between the two oceans.

1539 Negroes accompanied De Soto on his journey to the Mississippi. Estevanico, Negro companion of Spanish explorers, reached Arizona and New Mexico.

1540 The second settler in the State of Alabama was a Negro who was with De Soto's band. He remained and settled among the Indians.

1565 Negroes accompanied Mendez in founding St. Augustine, Florida.

1619 History of Negroes in English America began with landing of "twenty negars" at Jamestown, Virginia, in August.

1620 First public school for Negroes and Indians was established in Virginia.

1624 William Tucker was the first Negro child born and baptized in English America at Jamestown, Virginia. Tucker is said to have lived 108 years.

1638 First Negro slaves were brought into New England.

1688 First formal protest against slavery in Western Hemisphere made by Germantown Quakers at monthly meeting.

1704 Elias Nau, a Frenchman, opened the first school for Negroes in New York City.

1731 Benjamin Banneker was born near Baltimore, Maryland.

1750 Crispus Attucks escaped from his master in Farmingham, Mass.

1753 Scipio Moorehead, earliest known Negro artist, born.

Lemuel Haynes, first Negro to serve as a pastor in a white Congregation in United States, born July 18th.

1758 Frances Williams, first Negro college graduate in Western Hemisphere, published Latin poems.

1760 Richard Allen, founder and Bishop of the African Methodist Church, born a slave near Philadelphia.

1762 James Derham, who was born a slave in Philadelphia in 1762, is generally recognized as the first Negro physician in America.

1770 Crispus Attucks was first of five persons killed in Boston Massacre, March 5. He is generally regarded as first martyr of the Revolution.

1773 Massachusetts slaves petitioned legislature for freedom. There is a record of eight petitions during the Revolutionary War Period.

1774 First anti-slavery society organized in Philadelphia with Benjamin Franklin as president.

1775 Negro soldiers fought with distinction in the Battle of Bunker Hill. Peter Salem, a Negro, shot down Major Pitcairn and was one of the heroes of the day.

1776 Phillis Wheatley was invited by General Washington to visit him at his headquarters in Cambridge, Mass., so that he might express appreciation for her poems written in his honor.

1777 Vermont became the first American state to abolish slavery.

1780 Pennsylvania passed a law for the gradual abolition of slavery.

1787 The African Free School opened in New York City.

1790 Jean Baptiste Point deSable, French speaking Negro from Santo Domingo, established first permanent settlement at Chicago.

1792 Antoine Blanc founded the first Negro Catholic sisterhood in the United States.

1794 Richard Allen organized African Methodist Episcopal Church.

1808 Federal law barring the African slave trade went into effect.

1809 Negroes of Philadelphia organized African Baptist Church.

1814 New York Legislature authorized the formation of two Negro regiments.

1820 Harriet Tubman born a slave on a plantation in Dorchester County, Maryland.

1826 Ira Aldridge made London debut in Othello.

1827 Slavery was officially abolished in New York State.

1831 William Lloyd Garrison printed first issue of the *Liberator*, his abolitonist newspaper.

1834 Henry Blair was the first Negro to receive a patent for an invention - a corn harvester.

1836 Theodore S. Wright was the first Negro to receive a degree from a theological Seminary in U.S.

1838 First Negro periodical, *Mirror of Freedom* began publication in New York City.

1845 Macon B. Allen was the first Negro formally admitted to the Bar in Worcester, Massachusetts.

1847 Frederick Douglass began to publish the *North Star* newspaper on December 3rd in Rochester, New York.

1853 Lincoln University was chartered as Ashmond Institute in Chester, Pennsylvania, on January 1st. First Negro college in U.S.

1858 Daniel Hale Williams was born in Hollidaysburg, Pennsylvania.

1860 178,975 Negro soldiers in Union Army. Sixteen Negro soldiers received Congressional Medals of Honor for gallantry in action. One out of every four Union sailors was a Negro.

1861 Hampton Institute began its first day with Mary S. Peake as the first Negro teacher.

1862 U.S. Senate passed bill abolishing slavery in District of Columbia.

1863 President Lincoln signed Emancipation Proclamation, freeing the slaves.

1865 13th Amendment became part of U.S. Constitution.

1866 First Civil Rights Bill passed by Congress.

1869 Jefferson P. Long from Georgia was seated as the first Negro in the House of Representatives.

1870 Hiram R. Revels succeeded Jefferson Davis as U.S. Senator from Mississippi.

1872 John H. Conyers was the first Negro admitted to the U.S. Naval Academy.

1875 Blanche K. Bruce became member of U.S. Senate, representing Mississippi.

1877 Henry O. Flipper was the first Negro to graduate from West Point.

1881 Booker T. Washington opened Tuskegee Institute.

1886 First electric trolley on the American continent was run by a Negro, L. Clark Brooks.

1893 Dr. Daniel Hale Williams performed world's first successful heart operation at Chicago's Provident Hospital.

1896 National Association of Colored Women organized in Washington, D.C., by Dr. Mary Church Terrell.

1907 Alaine L. Locke of Harvard was the first American Negro Rhodes Scholar.

1909 NAACP founded on Lincoln's Birthday.

1912 W.C.Handy published the first blues composition, *Memphis Blues*.

1914 The Spingarn Medal awards were instituted by Joel E. Spingarn, Chairman of the Board of Directors of the NAACP, to call to the attention of the American people the existence of distinguished merit and achievement among black Americans.

1916 Major Charles Young received Spingarn Medal for services in Liberia.

1917 Julius Rosenwald Fund for Education, Scientific, and Religious Purposes was organized.

1918 The first two soldiers in the American Army to be decorated for bravery in France were Negroes named Henry Johnson and Needham Roberts.

1922 The Negro Renaissance reached its peak in the 20's.

1923 First Catholic seminary for the education of Negro priests was dedicated in Bay St. Louis, Mississippi.

1925 Adelbert H. Robert was elected to the Illinois State Legislature. He was the first Negro elected since reconstruction days.

1928 Oscar de Priest was the first Negro from a non-southern state to be elected to Congress.

1929 Brotherhood of Sleeping Car Porters received their Charter from the A.F. of L.

1930 *Green Pastures* opened on Broadway featuring Richard B. Harrison as "De Lawd."

1933 NAACP made its first attack on segregation and discrimination in education when it filed a suit against the University of North Carolina.

1936 Jesse Owens won four gold medals at the Berlin Olympics.

1937 William H. Hastie was confirmed as Judge of Federal District Court in the Virgin Islands. He became the first Negro federal Judge.

1939 Marian Anderson gave her Easter Sunday Open Air Recital in Washington, D.C.

1942 A group of Negro and white men and women, who were committed to direct nonviolent action, organized CORE, the Congress of Racial Equality in Chicago.

1943 The "Booker T. Washington", an American merchant ship, was launched. The helmsman was a Negro, Captain Malzoc.

1944 Adam Clayton Powell was the first Negro elected to Congress from the East.

1947 Jackie Robinson joined the Brooklyn Dodgers as the first Negro in organized baseball to play in the major leagues.

1948 Ralph J. Bunche was dispatched by the United Nations Secruity Council to mediate a border dispute between Palestine and its Arab neighbors.

1949 Congressman William L. Dawson approved as chairman of House Expenditures Committee. He was the first Negro to head a standing committee of Congress.

1950 Ralph J. Bunche, former U.N. Mediator in the Palestine dispute, awarded Nobel Peace Prize.

Gwendolyn Brooks, a young Chicago school teacher, won the Pulitzer Prize for her volume of poetry, *Annie Allen*.

1951 Pfc. William Thompson of Brooklyn won the Congressional Medal of Honor posthumously for heroism in Korea. He was the first Negro so honored since the Spanish-American War.

1952 Tuskegee Institute reported that 1952 was the first year in 71 years of tabulations that no lynchings were reported.

1954 U.S. Supreme Court, in an epochal decision, ruled that racial discrimination in public schools was unconstitutional.

1955 Marian Anderson made her debut on January 7th at Metropolitan Opera House as Ulrica in Verdi's *Masked Ball*. She was the first Negro singer in the company's history.

1956 U.S. Supreme Court banned segregation in public parks, playgrounds, beaches, and golf courses. The court rejected the "separate but equal" doctrine which had been previously passed.

1960 Student Non-Violent Coordinating Committee (S.N.C.C.) was formed at North Carolina's Shaw University.

1961 Robert Weaver sworn in as Administrator of the Housing and Home Finance Agency, highest federal post ever held by an American Negro.

1962 President Kennedy signed an executive order barring racial and religious discrimination in federally financed housing.

1963 President Kennedy calls for action to end segregation in a historic declaration affirming that segregation is a moral issue.

1964 Dr. Martin Luther King won the Nobel Peace Prize and thereby became the second American Negro in history to be so honored. Dr. Bunche was an earlier recipient.

1965 President Johnson signed a voting rights act allowing for federal registrars in Southern polling places, the action following a dramatic four day, 50 mile march from Selma to Montgomery, Alabama, led by Dr. Martin King.

1966 Edward Brooke was elected Senator from Massachusetts by popular vote.

1967 Thurgood Marshall became the first Negro appointed to a Supreme Court Judgeship.

1968 Martin Luther King, Jr., martyred by an assassin's bullet on April 4th, 1968, at approximately 6:01 P.M. Eastern Standard Time in Memphis, Tennessee. Dr. King died immediately.

1969 Charles Evers wins the race for mayor in his home town in Mississippi.

1970 Kenneth Gibson was elected mayor of Newark.

AFRO-AMERICAN CONTRIBUTORS

I. ABOLITIONISTS:

Frederick Douglass - (1817-1895) - A slave who became a great orator in the fight for freedom.

Henry Highland Garnet - (1815-1882) - Minister to Liberia - advocate of a slave revolt.

William Still - (1821-1902) - Underground Railroad Station Leader. Helped 649 slaves to freedom-station near Philadelphia. Secretary for the Pennsylvania Society for the Abolition of Slavery and Chairman from 1851-1861.

Mary Church Terrell - (1863-1954) - Entire life fought for equality. Lived in Washington and fought for end of segregation.

Sojourner Truth - (1797-1885) - A slave who became the first Negro orator to speak out against slavery.

II. ARMED SERVICES:

Brigadier General Benjamin O. Davis, Sr. - (1877----) - First Negro achieved through field promotions.

Major General Benjamin O. Davis, Jr. - (1912----) - West Point Graduate. Winner of the Distinguished Flying Cross and Silver Star for personal bravery. First Negro to command an air base.

Henry O. Flipper - First Negro to graduate from West Point. Graduated in 1877, but was only in service until 188l.

Charles Young - (1864-1922) - First Negro graduate of West Point to achieve distinction in the military. Entered 1884. Graduated in 1889. Active military career, rose to Colonel, went to Mexico, Haiti, Liberia, Cuba-trained soldiers during World War I. Sent to Liberia as Military Attache. Died in Africa, buried at Arlington.

III. BUSINESS:

Arthur G. Gaston - (1892----) - Millionaire. President and owner of an insurance company, a chain of 14 funeral homes, a business college, and cemetery in Birmingham, Alabama.

John H. Johnson - (1918----) - Publishes Ebony, Jet, Negro Digest and Tan. Combined circulation of nearly 2 million copies. Started Ebony as backbone of Johnson Publishing Company.

William Alexander Leidesdorff - (1810-1848) - Ship captain,trader,Americandiplomat,merchant,citytreasurer of San Francisco, owner of 35,000 acres of land near Sutter's Mill (Gold Rush). Died at 38. Left an estate of $1,500,000.

Anthony Overton - (1864-1946) - Ex-slave, judge, newspaper publisher, banker, and manufacturer, Overton-Hygenic Products Co. - baking powder, flavor extracts, toiletries. Harmon Award, 1927. Spingarn Medal, 1929. Started Victory Mutual Life Insurance Company which is still in business.

IV. EDUCATORS:

Mary McLeod Bethune - (1875-1955) - A Founder and President of Bethune-Cookman College.

Charlotte Hawkins Brown - (1884-1961) - Founder of Palmer Memorial Institute in North Carolina in 1902.

Wilhelmina Marguerita Crosson - (1902----) - Born in Rutherford, New Jersey. B.S. in Education from Boston Teachers College, Mass., in 1937. Author of numerous articles about education. Assistant to president, Palmer Memorial Institute, Sedalia, North Carolina.

V. CIVIL RIGHTS:

James Farmer - (1920----) - Born in Marshall, Texas, on January 12th. First National-Director of CORE, 1941-

65. President of Center for Community Action and Education, Inc., in Washington, D.C. 1966.

Dr. Martin Luther King, Jr. - (1929-1968) - Widely known clergyman and civil rights leader. Winner of Nobel Peace Prize in 1964 at age of 35.

Floyd H. McKissick - Current National President of CORE (Congress of Racial Equality).

Asa Philip Randolph - Organizer of the Brotherhood of Sleeping Car Porters, the strongest labor group among Negroes. Vice-President of AFL in 1957.

Roy Wilkins - Leader in the modern freedom movement. Executive Secretary of NAACP.

Whitney Young, Jr. - Social worker and civil rights leader. Executive Director of the Urban League.

VI. ENTERTAINMENT

A. ACTORS AND ACTRESSES:

Ossie Davis - (1917----). Born in Cogdell, Georgia, on December 18th. Graduate of Howard in 1939. Married Ruby Dee. Author and star of "Purlie Victorious" - play and film.

Sidney Poitier - 1963 Academy Award for best performance by an actor during the year.

Paul Robeson - (1898----) - Famous singer. Was famous athlete. Phi Beta Kappa at Rutgers. Obtained law degree from Columbia Law School. Turned to acting in 1921. Gave first concert in 1925. Popular recording artist. Spent many years in Russia.

Ethel Waters - (1900----) - Stage actress. Made debut in 1927. Mature and sensitive actress.

Bert Williams - (1878-1922) - From 1902 until death - the most famous Negro entertainer in America - comedian.

B. BAND LEADERS:

Count Basie - (1906----). (William). Born Red Bank, New Jersey, on August 21st. Musician in theaters, hotels, night clubs. Began as pianist with Benny Moten Band in 1929.

Duke Ellington - (1899----) - (Edward Kennedy). Born Washington, D.C. on April 29th. Composer. First professional appearance in 1916. First New York appearance in 1922. National recognition. Creative.

C. COMEDIANS AND COMEDIENNES:

Godfrey Cambridge - Accomplished Actor with a flair for comedy. Performed on Broadway in "The Blacks" and "Purlie Victorious." Comedian whose comments on the racial situation spares neither the Negro or the whites.

Bill Cosby - TV, night clubs. First Negro to have a starring role in a continuing dramatic series. Comic material is entirely non-racial.

Dick Gregory - (1932----) - Born in St. Louis, Missouri. Comedian, civil rights leader. Writes own satire monologues which point out, in mockery style, the wrongs that need righting in the U.S.

Jackie Moms Mabley - Down to earth performer in her 60's. In show business for the last 40 years.

Nipsey Russell - Television, night club and hotel performer. Writes short humorous poems.

D. COMPOSERS:

W. C. Handy - (1873-1958) - "Father of the Blues". Contributed to modern music. "St. Louis Blues".

VII. EXPLORERS:

Estevanico (Little Stephen) - One of four men to live through the expedition of Narverez. Spanish explorer, 1527, in Arizona and New Mexico.

Jean Baptiste de Sable - (1745-1845) - First settler of Chicago in 1772. Born in Haiti, Educated in France. Came to America in 1765. Fur trader. Traveled throughout America.

VIII. FINE ARTS:

James Baldwin - (1924----) - Born August 24th in New York City. Author. 1953, "Go Tell It On The Mountain". Developed huge following, thousands of readers of all races. Stated, "I want to be an honest man and a good writer."

William Edward Burghart DuBois - (1868-1963) - First editor of "Crisis." Stresses training of the Negro in liberal arts humanities. One of founders of NAACP in 1908. Scholar, spokesman, writer.

Zora Neal Hurston - Prolific but neglected author of 1930's and 40's. "Their Eyes Were Watching God". "Moses, Man of The Mountain."

LeRoi Jones - Two plays produced in 1965 - "The Toilet" and "The Slave." "The Dutchman" earlier won critical acclaim. Black Arts Theatre Project - part of cultural program of the Schomberg Collection of Negro Literature. Author of "Dead Lecturer" in 1964, collection of poems in jazz idiom.

IX. GOVERNMENT:

E. Frederic Morrow - (1909----) - Born in New Jersey. Educated at Bowdoin College and Rutgers University. 1955 was as Administrative Assistant to President Eisenhower. 1965 - Assistant Vice President of Bank of America International.

Carl Thomas Rowan - (1925----) - Born in Tennessee. Educated at Tennessee A. and I. College, Oberlin, and The University of Minnesota. 1964-65 Director of the U.S. Information Agency - supervised 12,000 employees in 106 countries. Former newspaper man and Ambassador to Finland. Currently affiliated with Chicago Daily News as Washington columnist.

William L. Dawson - (1886----) - Second Negro elected to Congress on Democratic ticket (from Illinois). Chairman of Government Operations Committee, elected 1943-1967.

Adam Clayton Powell, Jr. - (1908----) - Born in New Haven, Connecticut. Educated at Colgate University. 1945, elected to represent the New York's 18th Congressional District. Served as Chairman of the House Committee on Education and Labor.

Thurgood Marshall - (1908----) - Born in Baltimore, Maryland. Educated at Lincoln and Harvard Universities. 1965, U.S. Solicitor General. 1967, First Negro Judge in Supreme Court.

Edward Brooks - First Negro elected by popular vote as Senator from Massachusetts.

X. CLERGYMEN:

Richard Allen - (1760-1831) - Founder of the African Methodist Episcopal Church in 1787. Now oldest and largest institution among Negroes.

Richard H. Cain - (1825-1887) - Representative to Congress from South Carolina, 1873-1875, and 1877-1879. Methodist minister. 100,000 joined Methodist Church in South Carolina under his influence. Bishop of A.M.E. Church from 1880 until death in 1887.

Absalom Jones - Worked with Protestant Episcopal congregation. Formed a Negro military unit in the War of 1812. First Negro Grand Master of Masonry in the U.S.

Malcolm X - Died February 28, 1965, in New York City at age 39. Black Nationalist leader, former top aide of Elijah Muhammed.

Elijah Muhammed - Born Elijah Poole in Sandersville, Georgia, October 10, 1897. Worked as a field hand, railroad laborer, before moving to Detroit. In 1930, met the founder of the Nation of Islam (Black Muslims). Took over leadership of Black Muslims in 1934.

XI. SPORTS:

Jimmy Brown - Played for Cleveland Browns. Now retired. Born Manhasset, New York on February 17, 1936. Attended Syracuse University, where he received national recognition for his achievements in college football.

Cassius Clay - 1960 Olympics in Rome, was light-heavyweight winner. Won heaveyweight championship from Sonny Liston on February 25, 1964, by K.O. in 7th round. World Boxing Association withdrew recognition as champion in 1966.

Jesse Owens - Athlete of year in 1936 for Track and Field. Elected in 1950 as the top athlete for half a century in track and field. 1936 Olympics - won 100 meter run, 200 meter run, 400 meter relay, and the long jump - 4 gold medals.

Wilma Rudolph Ward - Athlete of the year in 1960 and 1961. 1961 Amateur Athlete of the Year. 1960 Olympics, Rome; won 100 meter run, 200 meter run and 400 meter relay team events - 3 gold medals.

Hank Aaron - right-fielder for Atlanta Braves.

Roy Campanella - Catcher for Dodgers. Paralyzed in automobile accident at peak of career.

Elston Howard - catcher for Yankees. First Negro in Yankee organization. Traded to Boston Red Sox in 1967.

Don Newcombe - Most valuable player, 1956. Pitcher, 1956, Cy Young Award as the Major League Pitcher of the Year. (First year for the award).

Wilt Chamberlain - (Wilton). Philadelphia Warriors, 1959-1962; San Francisco, 1962-64; Philadelphia, 1965-66. Scoring champion, 1959-65.

INDEX

Words found here in boldface type represent the entire chapter for each of the Afro-Americans included in the book.

accomplishments, 9
agricultural, 70
almanac, 7, 9, 11
Anderson, Marian, 140-147
astronomy, 9
athletic, 152
autobiography, 17

Baltimore, 10, 11, 15, 16
Banneker, Benjamin, 6-13
Bethune, Mary Mcleod, 98-105
Bethune-Cookman College, 100, 103
blizzards, 79
Boston Symphony Orchestra, 84
Bunche, Ralph, 130-139

Canada, 31
Carver, George Washington, 64-73
champion, 150
chemist, 107
chemistry, 108
Chesapeake Bay, 11
choir, 141
Civil War, 20
Cleveland, Grover, 50, 53
clock, 7, 8, 10
cobbler, 35
college, 99
Columbia University, 116
Columbian Orator, 18
competitive, 126
conductor, 28
consul, 84
constellations, 10
contestant, 152
contract, 172

DePauw University, 108, 110, 111
demonstrations, 163
Douglass, Frederick, 14-23
Drew, Charles, 122-129
Dunbar, Paul Laurence, 90-97

Edison, Thomas A., 71
elementary, 132
Emancipation Proclamation, 20, 94
Eskimos, 76, 79

Fisk University, 85, 108, 110
floes, 79
Ford, Henry, 71
Freeman's Hospital, 53

Gandhi, Mohandis, 162
Garrison, William Lloyd, 19
Giants, San Francisco, 167

Haiti, 119
Hampton Institute, 41, 42, 45
Harvard University, 111, 133
Henson, Matthew, 74-81
hospital, 49, 50, 53, 124
Howard University, 135
Hughes, Langston, 114-121

Jefferson, Thomas, 11
Johnson, James Weldon, 82-89
Julian, Percy, 106-113

King, Martin Luther Jr., 158-165

laboratory, 67, 123, 127
league, 168
Library of Congress, 95
Lincoln, Abraham, 20
Lincoln Memorial, 141, 145, 161, 163
Lindsay, Vachel, 120

Matzeliger, Jan E., 34-39
Mays, Willie Howard, 166-175
Memphis, Tenn., 161, 164
Metropolitan Opera, 143
Missionary School, 102
Mississippi River, 119

Nobel Peace Prize, 131, 133, 136, 161
North Pole, 75
North Star, 17, 20
North Star, 25

pharmaceutical, 111
Philadelphia Academy of Fine Arts, 60
plantation, 16
plasma, 124, 127
protest, 160
Provident Hospital, 50, 53

Robinson, Jackie, 148-157
Rochester, New York, 20, 31
Rochester, University of, 71

Southern Christian Leadership Conference, 163
sun, 7, 9
supervise, 45
Swarthmore College, 135

Tanner, Henry Ossawa, 56-63
temperatures, 79
transfusions, 127
trophies, 101
Tubman, Harriet, 24-33
Tuskegee Institute, 41, 43, 46, 67, 70

Underground Railroad, 28, 30
United Nations, 131, 133, 136,

valedictorian, 134
vocational school, 43

Washington, Booker T., 40-47
Washington, D.C., 7, 9, 11, 12
Washington, George, 9, 11
Williams, Daniel Hale, 48-55

ACKNOWLEDGMENTS

Acknowledgment is made to the following for permission to reproduce the art and photographs that appear on the pages indicated:

Associated Publishers, 6, 34

Explorer's Club, 74

Historical Pictures Service, 14, 24, 40, 48, 56, 64, 82, 90, 98, 114

Johnson Publishing Co., 122, 130, 140, 148, 158, 166

Ranft, Max, Cover, 9, 17, 27, 36, 43, 51, 59, 67, 77, 85, 93, 101, 109, 117, 125, 133, 143, 151, 161, 169

Edited by: John P. Quirk

SUBJECT AREA CORRELATION CHART

BIOGRAPHIES	SOCIAL STUDIES	LANGUAGE ARTS
PAUL LAURENCE DUNBAR	Contribution: Author of 2 books of poetry	Poetry Study of card catalogue and library procedures
MARY McLEOD BETHUNE	Contribution: Started first school for Negroes	Writing Biographies
PERCY LANON JULIAN	Living together in different communities Citizenship	Write "tall tales" about scientists
LANGSTON HUGHES	Contribution: Wrote poetry	Book Week Poetry — write a poem and set it to music
CHARLES DREW	Contribution: Pioneer in preserving blood (plasma)	Write stories about the life of Dr. Drew
RALPH BUNCHE	Contribution: Delegate to U.N. Honors: Nobel Peace Prize	Research and write about Nobel Peace Prize
MARIAN ANDERSON	Contribution: First Negro to sing in Metropolitan Opera	Listening Biographies
JACKIE ROBINSON	Community Relations Contribution: First Negro to play major league baseball	Study and write about Baseball Hall of Fame
MARTIN LUTHER KING, JR.	Contribution: Civil Rights Movement Honor: Nobel Peace Prize	Debates Reports Analyze newspaper stories on civil rights
WILLIE MAYS	Honors: Most Valuable Player 1954 and 1964	Write original stories on sports and sports figures